Dr. Tashiera Howard

"This dissertation is a profound and timely exploration of a complex and sensitive topic: the intersection of church teachings, pastoral care, and the phenomenon of suicide. Dr. Bracy has approached this deeply challenging subject with both academic rigor and compassionate insight, offering a nuanced analysis that bridges theology, psychology, and pastoral practice. Through meticulous research and thoughtful interpretation, the dissertation sheds light on how faith communities can better understand and support individuals struggling with suicidal thoughts. It highlights the church's potential role not just as a moral guide but as a source of solace and hope, emphasizing the importance of empathy, open dialogue, and informed pastoral care. The author's ability to navigate the theological, ethical, and practical dimensions of this topic is commendable. The work challenges preconceptions, addresses stigma, and provides valuable recommendations for church leaders, mental health professionals, and believers alike. This dissertation stands as an important contribution to both academic scholarship and the ongoing efforts of faith communities to respond with compassion and understanding to the realities of mental health crises."

Christopher White, LPC, LLC

"*Suicide Among Kingdom Believers in the Black Church: What the Saints Aren't Testifying About,* is a groundbreaking exploration of mental health within the Black church, offering a compassionate and insightful perspective on a topic often shrouded in stigma. Dr. Curtis T. Bracy masterfully intertwines theological insights with psychological research, making the book both informative and relatable. His dedication to addressing the emotional struggles of Black men and the importance of open dialogue is commendable, providing a much-needed resource for clergy and congregants alike. What a great work that can open the door to making suicide a constant topic of discussion within the church arena."

Consulted By:

LIGHTHOUSE
CONSULTING

A Division of Carr Corp Enterprises, LLC
www.ashericarr.com

SUICIDE AMONG KINGDOM BELIEVERS IN THE BLACK CHURCH

WHAT THE SAINTS AREN'T TESTIFYING ABOUT

CURTIS T. BRACY, C.PsyD, LMFCT

What The People Are Saying About *Suicide Among Kingdom Believers in the Black Church: What the Saints Aren't Testifying About*

Dr. Chelece Brown

"*Suicide Among Kingdom Believers in the Black Church* is an essential and thought-provoking work that addresses a long-overdue conversation about mental health within the African-American church community. The book provides a candid look at how suicide and mental health struggles are often neglected or silenced in faith-based environments, particularly within Black churches where spirituality is central to healing. Dr. Bracy offers not only an exploration of why these issues are rarely discussed but also presents practical steps for breaking the silence. As a suicide attempt survivor, I understand the isolation that comes from feeling like there is no safe space to share your struggles, especially in places meant for healing and community. Dr. Bracy's book gives voice to those who are hurting in silence, showing that faith and mental health care can coexist. This work is crucial for pastors, congregants, and mental health professionals, as it calls for a shift in the way we approach mental health in faith communities, urging us to make room for the full spectrum of human experience, including pain, depression, and thoughts of suicide."

Whitney Warr, LPC (Licensed Professional Counselor)

"Dr. Bracy's book, *Suicide Among Kingdom Believers*, was an excellent read—informative, well-written, and thoroughly supported by research and facts. As both a therapist and a follower of Christ, I deeply appreciated the insights shared. The church often lacks education on the topic of suicidal ideation, which can prevent people from receiving the holistic help they need—both spiritually and naturally. The book is filled with passion and conviction, addressing not only suicide but also related struggles. This book is essential for all churches and should be required reading for church leaders to continue the vital movement of suicide education within the church."

Content Warning

This book contains the following sensitive topics:

Abuse, neglect & abandonment
Anxiety disorders & anxiety attacks
Body shaming
Cheating
Depression
Drug abuse
Mental illness
Panic attacks
Rape
Sexual abuse
Suicide
Verbal abuse

Some topics may bring up thoughts and emotions that can
be overwhelming and should be tackled under the guidance
of mental health or other support professionals.

DEDICATION

I dedicate this book to the love of my life and gorgeous wife, Lady Shadae Bracy. Thank you for all the support and encouragement while completing my dissertation. Thank you for choosing to take this journey with me. To my bundle of joy and beautiful daughter Zion, Daddy loves you so much. Seeing you laugh and play keeps me going. I dedicate this book to the memory of my grandmother, Pastor Anna Cooper, who is gone but never forgotten.

This book is also dedicated to my mother, Prophetess Loria Bracy. Thank you for always telling me to dream big and never settle. I want to also dedicate this book to my father in the gospel, Bishop Mark E. Parrott, Sr. Thank you so much for believing in the call of Christ our King on my life. You have truly exemplified on and off camera how clergy should live before Christ and His people.

Next, I dedicate this book to my Lighthouse Temple Church family. Thank you all for supporting my Kingdom ministry and publications. I hope you will enjoy this one as well.

—Dr. Curtis T. Bracy, C.PsyD

Contents

INTRODUCTION

I have always had a keen interest in studying and researching topics that were seldom discussed from the pulpit. I grew up in the church, specifically in the Pentecostal denomination, and later in the Apostolic-Pentecostal denomination. I never heard a sermon addressing the Biblical topic of suicide. The only thing mentioned about suicide was where those who commit it go when they die.

Being of African American descent and growing up in what is considered "the Black Church," many people of color at the time could not afford therapy, nor did we have insurance. More importantly, African Americans, to a large degree, did not believe in seeing a mental health professional. When asked why, the responses ranged from "I believe in God" to "You know Black people don't do that! We go to church."

In fact, I remember one of my grandmother's friends who passed away never went to the doctor for her physical ailments because she believed Christ would heal her. She passed away in 2002, never having seen a doctor. Not only did many Kingdom believers of color avoid addressing their physical health when I was growing up, they ignored their mental health as well. I recall hearing the older saints sing songs like "He has kept me from all evil with my mind stayed on Jesus." While their minds were on Jesus, they also taught themselves to suppress unresolved and untreated trauma. This was deeply disturbing to me.

The same Jesus who gave us medical physicians also provided mental health professionals. I have always had a love for the Bible. However, my love for studying psychology was just as great. Still, the Bible has the final say over psychology, just as Christ has the last word over what medical doctors say. I began meticulously studying psychology in 2007 after my own bouts with depression. Up until that time, I hadn't heard any sermons addressing depression, anxiety, or other mental health struggles. Then, the Lord Jesus put that passion in my heart to address it.

After I started addressing topics like depression, anxiety, unhealthy self-worth, and various mental health struggles, I began to see parishioners come to me directly after service with questions about what I had addressed from the Bible concerning the mental health issues they were facing. Additionally, I started receiving phone calls from church members who were battling depression, anxiety, and even thoughts of suicide or suicidal attempts. However, I was not trained to address their suicidal thoughts. All I knew was the common belief that Christians who commit suicide go to hell.

First, I had to confront my own bias about the thought of a Kingdom believer wanting to commit suicide. It's easy to assume that all a person has to do is have faith and everything will be alright—until you're confronted with your own struggles. Secondly, I wanted to educate myself as much as possible on the topic of suicide. I began watching documentaries, reading books by psychologists, psychiatrists, and licensed professional coun-selors. After obtaining my Master's in counseling and passing the National Counselor Exam (NCE), I wanted to take it a step further.

I became certified in neuropsychotherapy (NPT-C), EMDR-II (Eye Movement Desensitization and Reprocessing), and crisis counseling & suicide prevention. Lastly, I earned my Doctorate from Christian Bible Institute & Seminary in Christian Counseling and Psychology (CPsy.D). I chose to write my disser-tation on suicide among Kingdom believers in the Black church for several reasons: from my experience with parishioners who struggled with suicidal thoughts, to emphasize the importance of breaking the silence on suicide in the body of Christ—specif-ically in the Black church—and to provide a clinical counseling and psychology publication from a Kingdom Biblical perspec-tive, citing evidence-based research. I also wanted to highlight the importance of understanding the "Black psychology" of the Black church and how we typically respond to trauma and emotional distress.

While the topic of suicide among Christians is broad, this publication will focus on the silence surrounding suicide in local churches and national organizations within the Black church. It will also address why the church remains silent on this issue and how we can break that silence. Lastly, we will examine the topic from both a Biblical and clinical perspective, demonstrating the importance of Christians seeking treatment while trusting in Jesus Christ, our King of kings and Lord of lords, at the same time. It is my prayer that this work will forever revolutionize your life and help break your silence as well.

CHAPTER ONE

The Phone Call

"We all need somebody to lean on."
—Bill Withers

I finally had a chance to sit down and relax. Just when I thought it would be a typical night, the phone rang. I wasn't surprised by the number on the caller ID, but I was shocked by the parishioner's presenting problem:

> "Please don't tell anyone, but I've been thinking about killing myself."

Her presenting problem shocked me for two reasons. First, it didn't match her outward appearance. It's often said, especially in dating, "When you're meeting someone, you're not really meeting them; you're meeting their representative." The same could be said in many of our church settings. This woman knew how to look the part on Sunday morning. Outwardly, she made sure not an ounce of suicidal thoughts slipped through her church smile or her engagement in worship. Yet, the façade was only adding to her pain, creating more emotional wounds. This kind of disconnect is all too common in the Black church.

Secondly, I was shocked because, up until this phone call, I had no formal training in suicide prevention, nor was I trained to assist people in crisis. The only thing I was equipped to do as a sincere preacher was to pray with the parishioner and offer them some Scriptures to quote. In that moment, all I could think to do was ask her questions based on what I already knew about her. I had been counseling her for several weeks, but the topic of suicide had never come up. Those first few counseling sessions were what the counseling profession calls "building rapport," which focuses on establishing the therapeutic alliance.

The Danger of the Uneducated Preacher

While I had learned a few counseling skills, I was still an undergraduate at Kean University, studying psychology. None of the preachers in the church I attended were educated in counseling. We just prayed and encouraged the congregants to have faith in God. Interestingly, not one class in my undergraduate program covered suicide—not a single discussion, lecture, or assignment on the topic. So, I made up my mind that before I counseled anyone else with suicidal thoughts, I was going to get educated.

I was determined to finish graduate school and obtain my master's in counseling with a specialization in marriage, family, and couples counseling. However, the topic of suicide never left the forefront of my mind. Every clinician in the counseling profession has their niche, and I felt ignited with a passion and a prompting from King Jesus Christ to make three areas my central focus: low self-esteem, trauma (from a neuropsychotherapy perspective), and suicidality. I wanted to make an academic impact and contribute to the Black church, the broader church, and the world at large by addressing the topic of suicide among Kingdom believers. For this, education is crucial, especially for clergy.

In a statistical investigation conducted by the Institute of Social and Religious Research in 1935, findings revealed that out of 200,000 Protestant congregations in the United States and Canada, served by approximately 150,000 ministers, 50% had neither college nor seminary training.[1]

Furthermore, the study showed that 18% had college training only, and 12% had seminary training only. This leaves only 20% of Protestant ministers in North America with both a college education and post-graduate divinity school training.[2]

Additionally, there is a bias within the Black church—especially in Pentecostal organizations—that believes all one needs to preach is the Holy Spirit. Some will cite the apostle Peter, referring to him as "unschooled" (Acts 4:13, NIV). However, what's often overlooked is that Peter was a Jewish man. All Jewish men in Peter's time were familiar with the Tanakh by the time of their bar mitzvah.[3] While Peter's confession that King Jesus was "the Christ, the Son of the living God" (Matthew 16:16, ESV) came from divine revelation from the Father (Matthew 16:17), his knowledge of the Torah came from his upbringing.

By the time Christ came to earth at His first advent, as Yahweh in the flesh, He expounded on the Law and the Prophets that Peter was already familiar with.

> *44 "He said to them, "This is what I told you while I was still with you: Everything must be fulfilled that is written about me in the Law of Moses, the Prophets and the Psalms." (Luke 24:44, NIV)*

Peter was so well acquainted with the Laws of Moses that Christ had to remind him of the Newer Covenant:

> *9 About noon the following day as they were on their journey and approaching the city, Peter went up on the roof to pray. 10 He became hungry and wanted something to eat, and while the meal was being prepared, he fell into a trance. 11 He saw heaven opened and something like a large sheet being let down to earth by its four corners. 12 It contained all kinds of four-footed animals, as well as reptiles and birds. 13 Then a voice told him, 'Get up, Peter. Kill and eat.' 14 'Surely not, Lord!' Peter*

> *replied. 'I have never eaten anything impure or unclean.' 15 The voice spoke to him a second time, 'Do not call anything impure that God has made clean.' (Acts 10:9-15, NIV)*

As one can see, Peter, while not seminary-trained, was well-versed in the Law and the Prophets to such a degree that it influenced how he viewed non-Jewish individuals—those Christ wanted Peter to preach to. Jewish boys were learning the Old Testament during their formative years. The Tanakh wasn't just their religion; it was their life. In contrast, in Western culture, religion is often forgotten by young adults by the time they go off to college. For others in America who are learning the Word of God, they are often receiving their teaching from uneducated clergy.

Even God Himself remarked that His people are destroyed for lack of knowledge (Hosea 4:6). Furthermore, not only do some clergy deny the necessity of seminary training, but they also harbor a bias against psychology and clinical counseling. In fact, an article from Western Conservative Baptist Seminary revealed findings in 1986 regarding this issue:

> Some Christians, however, are uncomfortable with psychology in its empirical form. For example, a recent issue of the Bible Science Newsletter, normally dedicated to promoting creationism, devoted an entire issue to critiquing psychology. Articles from this issue included 'The Failure of Modern Psychology' (Thorn, 1986), 'Why Bother With Psychology?' (Bartz, 1986), and 'Sensible Psychology: How Creation Makes the Difference' (Pearcy, 1986). These articles warn that modern psychology is not a science and that psychology is invalid since it relies on ways of knowing other than through authority (i.e., the Bible).[4]

While many believed there should be a clear
divide between the sacred and the secular, especially in counseling, the 1986 findings were a couple of years behind the start
of Biblical counseling, which began in the
1960s.[5] Interestingly enough, in the same
year—1986—the importance of Christian and
Biblical counseling was gaining traction. In
1986, Gary R. Collins founded the American
Association of Christian Counselors (AACC)
and became its first president.[6]

While we have come a long way in our theological views
regarding the integration of psychology and Biblical counseling, there still remains a stigma that mental illness should solely
be dealt with through prayer and memorizing Scriptures.[7] This
is concerning because the Bible, while being the sole authority
for Kingdom believers, does not provide detailed information on
everything. For example, the Bible does not give us information
on kidney failure, diabetes, or the signs of suicide. Therefore, we
trust the experts to whom Christ has given knowledge, through
education, to assist humanity—as long as their insights don't
contradict the Holy Scriptures.

While the Bible accentuates the historical fact and Kingdom
truth that King Jesus Christ is our Great Physician, we still go
to the emergency room when we have fevers and for our annual
checkups. By the same token, we must be just as concerned with
our mental health as we are with our physiological and theological health. Furthermore, some clergy believe that mental health
struggles are a matter of the heart, not the brain.[8] However,
there are many clergy who would disagree, and I am certainly
one of them.

In 2016, I came across what is called Neurocounseling. What
is that, you might ask? Neurocounseling is a newer branch of
mental health therapy that uses traditional approaches combined

with brain-based research to implement brain-based counseling interventions, changing the way the brain functions.[9]

Thankfully, other clergy are trained, educated, and certified, attempting to persuade the large number of clergy who deny its reality. Licensed clinical social worker, trauma therapist, and minister Dr. Anita Phillips postulates that "Emotions begin in the body, not the mind. We are embodied. There is no separation."[10] I wanted to learn the effects of trauma on the brain to better serve the sons and daughters of God, advancing the Kingdom of Christ.

After the terrorist attacks of September 11, 2001, the chronic racist acts brought to mainstream attention through technological advances like camera phones, and the post-COVID-19 pandemic crisis, secular mental health clinicians were encouraged to take CE (continued education) and become certified in trauma counseling. In fact, I took this seriously and developed a lifelong commitment to studying trauma and becoming certified in it as well. This is essential not only for secular clinicians but for Christian counselors as well.

A recent study conducted by the Center for Church and Community at Baylor University gathered responses from 331 pastors and clergy about their knowledge of trauma. Additionally, the survey looked at how their education equipped them to understand the trauma of their parishioners.[11] The study revealed that three-fourths (76%) reported that they were "somewhat prepared" or "very prepared" for trauma among their congregants, while only 24% reported being "somewhat prepared" or "unprepared."[12]

One of the greatest moments of ministry for me post-pandemic was sitting on panels within the church organization I'm affiliated with, providing clinical answers for trauma from a Christian counseling and psychology perspective. It is vital that clergy and pastors at large understand that while it's wonderful for members in their congregations to trust in their spiritual gifts, it's also a plus when congregants know you're educated and skilled to deal with their psychological wounds as well.

Trusting the Therapeutic Alliance

Trust is the foundation of leadership. When members feel like they can trust you, they will dedicate their time, resources, and even their lives to you. Moreover, trusting leadership with thoughts of suicide is equally vital. Many in our congregation struggle with mental health and keep it a secret from their pastors, even though they share everything else with them. Many in the body of Christ, who feel comfortable sharing good news like a child graduating from high school, a new job, or other blessings, will hesitate to share thoughts of suicide. In fact, a congregant who is suicidal may even act on it due to feeling they couldn't come to clergy for help.

It's also important to consider that many people choose their churches based on what they hear being addressed from the pulpit. Abaron Buer reported through his research that the top reason people chose the church they attend was because they loved the sermons.[13] The greater concern is whether preachers are addressing the sensitive but necessary topics. Since the Holy Scriptures contain the truth of God, we must ask ourselves: were these sensitive topics addressed in the Word of God? Dr. Frank Thomas emphasizes the importance of addressing sensitive issues in sermons:

> Many churches and preachers, including some Black churches and Black preachers, do not like to discuss violence, 'urban,' 'ghetto,' or big city problems. We do not like to discuss what Phyllis Tribble calls the 'texts of terror,' such as the violence against four women in ancient Israel: Hagar (Genesis 16:1-16), Tamar (2 Samuel 13:1-19), an unnamed concubine (Judges 19:1-30), and the daughter of Jephthah (Judges 11:1-40). We do not like to talk about the violence of human cruelty in the Bible, the apparent silence of God, and other

texts that sanction rape, conquest, genocide, slavery, assassination, beheading, and the like.[14]

The time has come for the church to address the issues that compromise mental health by confronting the unresolved pain of the masses in the pews. This is desperately needed in the Black church. While the above topics may be difficult to address from the pulpit on a Sunday morning, people are turning to other places and even other religions that boldly address them. Mental wellness matters to congregants. A myriad of sermons are based on the construct of the media-based simulation of the American dream.[15] Most of our pulpits in American churches are filled with messages about living "the American dream," while people of color are still processing the police brutality faced by George Floyd, Breonna Taylor, and Eric Garner.

The question is: can the members in the pews count on their clergy to tell the truth from a Biblical framework, emphasizing that King Jesus Christ cares about the whole person? After all, the apostle Peter encouraged us in the first century to cast all our cares on Christ because He cares for us (1 Peter 5:7). Since the church has failed to address these issues, many are turning away to what they deem as "real" in movies, television, entertainment, sports, money, sex, and the like.[16]

In both secular and Christian counseling, the therapeutic alliance is the foundation of counseling. Although scholars have different views on how the alliance is conceptualized, most theoretical definitions include three common themes: the collaborative nature of the relationship, the affective bond between patient and therapist, and their ability to agree on treatment goals and tasks.[17] Samuel Gladding defines the therapeutic alliance as "Two people in therapeutic contact. There are three common factors to an effective therapeutic alliance: a collaborative relationship, an affective bond, and an agreement on goals and tasks."[18]

The good news, however, is that many seminaries, Christian colleges, and universities are adding counseling and psychology courses to their curriculums to better equip clergy to present a psycho-theological message to their congregants. According to the research findings of Dr. Everett L. Worthington, Jr., "Religiously accommodated treatments had much greater spiritual effects on the patients than equivalent secular therapies and were better at increasing clients' spiritual lives than strictly similar secular treatments."[19]

One of my friends in ministry, Dr. Michael R. Jackson, shared that in his Christian private practice, he has counseled many who were not professing Christians, but after the pandemic, they were eager to know from clergy who were licensed Christian counselors: "What is God saying about my situation?"[20]

Prior to "The Phone Call"

As stated earlier in this chapter, I had been counseling this woman for some time. The topic of suicide never came up. She would usually discuss her marital problems, low self-esteem, childhood, and her current depression. We talked more about her depression than any other topic. Ironically, depression and suicide are intimately linked.[21] While not all depressed individuals are suicidal, depression can lead to intrusive suicidal thoughts.[22] This phone call taught me some important concepts that I highly recommend clergy and Christian counselors never forget:

> ➢ Being trained and skilled in crisis intervention and suicide prevention is crucial for clergy.
> ➢ Prayer is essential, but suicide risk assessments should be done at the onset of counseling.
> ➢ Quoting Scripture is appropriate, but only after first addressing the immediate crisis.
> ➢ Referrals are critical. Christian counselors are not licensed to prescribe medication or provide psychiatric care. A multidisciplinary team is pivotal in the counseling profession. If listening and counseling at that

moment doesn't seem effective, it's time to reach out to other professionals or even call 911.
➢ Follow-up is key. Never assume that a client or church member who survived a suicide attempt is "fine" simply because they stopped talking about it. Experts agree that this is still a serious concern.

SHE'S STILL ALIVE

By the grace of the Almighty King of Glory, the woman I was counseling is still alive and no longer wishes to die. Her marriage has improved, and her depressive symptoms have decreased. Her faith in Christ, her King, remains strong. She thanked me for being there for her, but what she will never fully understand is how her phone call changed the trajectory of how I approach mental health. It also fueled my desire to educate the Black church, and the church at large, on the mental health struggles of many believers who love the Lord Jesus but struggle to love themselves.

That phone call was much needed. When we spoke years later, I said to her, "Thank you for calling." Now, we must examine why so many congregants in the Black church aren't picking up the phone to reach out to clergy or their pastor for clinical Christian counseling.

RESEARCH QUESTIONS

The following Research questions align with my purpose statement, guiding this research project.

Research Question #1

Has the Black Church treated the topic of suicide as an isolated mental health issue due to religious views on the afterlife of individuals who commit suicide or have suicidal ideations? The tools used to collect data for this research question included completed questionnaires from pastors, clergy, and church members within the Black church..

Research Question #2

Do congregants in the Black church feel comfortable discussing their mental health or past and present thoughts of suicidal ideations with other members or clergy within the Black church? The tools used to collect data for this research question were completed surveys from members of the Black church..

Research Question #3

What do members of the Black church recommend incorporating in psychoeducation to raise awareness of suicidal ideations, behaviors, and warning signs so the Black church can launch, establish, and improve mental health fellowship, support, and prevention? The data for this research was collected through questionnaires completed by adults in the Black church who have experienced past suicidal thoughts and attempts. Additionally, interviews were conducted with licensed therapists of color who attend the Black church.

RATIONALE FOR THIS RESEARCH

The topic of suicide has seldom been discussed in the Black church, at least as far back as I can remember. While the Black church has made strides in hosting conferences, workshops, and Zoom calls on church growth and economic development, the psychology of people of color within the Black church is rarely addressed—especially suicide. Even in panels I've had the opportunity to sit on to discuss mental health in the Black church, ninety percent of them did not bring up the topic of suicide.

The reason suicide is often avoided isn't just because it's a sensitive subject. It's seldom discussed due to the church's views on where a person who dies by suicide goes after death. In staying silent on this topic to avoid offending congregants who may have had unsaved family members die by suicide, we neglect those in our congregations who are living with suicidal ideations.

With this research, I aim to equip the pulpits with awareness about what the pews in the Black church might be too embarrassed to tell them directly, but were able to express through surveys and questionnaires. Communication is key in the leadership of the Black church. Strategic leadership expert Dr. Khandicia Randolph argues in her research on Black church leadership that "trust is the bedrock of all relationships and is established through communication. The success of leadership starts with effective communication, much of which takes the form of non-verbal and expressive cues."[23]

But how can one communicate what they don't know or have a bias against? It's time for the church to address the elephant in the room. As Pastor Kenya Procter stated:

> In many Black communities, the church is often a hub for many services beyond spiritual uplift. In rural communities especially, congregants and non-congregants rely on churches for information about everything from voting to health care. It is also the first place many people bring their celebrations and their troubles, money struggles, and personal grief. So, **if clergy isn't talking about suicide, "then that means nobody's talking about it.**[24]

For decades, people of color have looked to the Black church for economic wellness, spiritual growth, and emotional assistance, but are just now learning to find comfort in addressing their mental health crises. If the only thing the church can do is condemn those who have died by suicide to hell, we will never address the mental health needs of those in our churches who aren't dead yet. After all, Christ our King made it clear that those who are not sick don't need a physician (Luke 5:31-32). In the same way, even those without mental health struggles in the Black church need to be educated, because life can be unmanageable and overwhelming—even for Kingdom-minded believers.

Many within the Black church are leaving because their psychoeducational and other needs are not being met. In fact, the Black church is losing young Black males to the Nation of Islam. Dr. Dana Carson, Apostle and founder of Reflections of Christ Kingdom International, explains this phenomenon:

> The Nation today has a strong respect in the community, because of the social programs that it offers in some urban communities. Henry notes that, 'The Nation of Islam runs counseling programs for prisoners, drug addicts, alcoholics, and street gang members, which they intentionally recruit. In addition to these intentional outreaches of the Nation of Islam, they also provide manhood training classes to teach the history of the Black man.[25]

It's vital for the Black church to remember that while we are busy running food pantries, there are many in our congregations who haven't eaten due to severe major depressive disorder. While we condemn those from the pulpit who haven't been to church for weeks, some clergy don't follow up but assume they've left the church. The reality may be that they felt no sense of community or fellowship and are planning to leave this life. If preachers or pastors allow their ego and insecurity to get in the way, the advancement of the Kingdom of Christ will be stunted by their failure to take mental health—particularly suicide—seriously.

REVIEW OF RELEVANT LITERATURE

The relevant literature consulted for this research consists of books, journal articles, and case studies by competent, proficient, and skilled authors in the fields of psychology, counseling, mental health, and suicide. The resources include both past and the most recent publications on this much-needed work. The themes addressed focus on the silence of the Black church regarding suicide, the lack of education on mental health and suicide among clergy, and the recommendations from faithful members of the Black church.

Furthermore, the literature review includes statistics gathered at the international, national, and state levels. These statistics will also reveal discrepancies between the white church and the Black church, the latter of which faces a higher suicide rate. Additionally, the research incorporates new studies by suicide expert Dr. Craig J. Bryan to distinguish between suicides stemming from mental illness and those driven by emotional distress. I also consulted websites that provided both historical and the most current literature on suicide at large and among Kingdom believers in the Black church. These firsthand experiences, along with the surveys and questionnaires, serve as a call for greater public awareness and support from the Black church.

The literature confirms the lack of education among Black pastors and clergy concerning suicidal ideation, attempts, warning signs, and prevention. I focus primarily on the work of suicide expert Dr. Bryan; African American mental health expert Dr. Pamela Robinson; Dr. Rheeda Walker, who has published over fifty scientific papers on African American adult mental health; Dr. Charles A. Moody, Jr., on the systemic racism experienced by people of color in America; Dr. Joy A. DeGruy, an internationally renowned researcher and educator on racism, trauma, and violence affecting people of color; Mary-Frances Winters, author of Black Fatigue; Dr. Jennifer Mullan, a leading expert and psychologist on Black decolonization; and Dr. Thema Bryant, former Black president of the American Psychological Association (APA). Lastly, the work of licensed clinical social worker Terrie M. Williams will be discussed in this research.

Book Overview

Chapter one introduces the passion behind this research, which all started with a phone call. After hanging up, I was left concerned about the caller and wondered how many other parishioners in the Black church were not reaching out due to the stigma and stereotype within the African American community—that people of color don't go to therapy, let alone discuss it with the Black church we faithfully attend and give our offerings to.

Chapter two delves into the relevant literature on this topic, addressing the silence in the Black church concerning mental health, particularly as it pertains to suicidal ideation, suicide attempts, and suicide survivors. Chapter three continues this conversation by exploring other ways in which the silence surrounding mental health manifests in self-destructive behaviors. Chapter four tackles the reservations that members of the Black church have about opening up to clergy and fellow congregants regarding their mental health, particularly when it comes to suicidal thoughts. Chapter five discusses practices and methods in the Black church that have not helped but instead contributed to the growing needs around suicidality in our communities.

Chapter six addresses the concern of King Jesus Christ for our minds, not just our physical bodies. Our psychology mattered to Christ as much as our physiology. Chapter seven focuses on how the mental health of Black men has often been neglected in the Black church, as the church tends to cater more to women while casting aside Black men. Chapter eight highlights the importance of meeting the Black church where they are concerning their mental health. Chapter nine emphasizes Christ our King and how He dealt with mental health and emotional distress during His first advent. This chapter will also explore the distinction between emotional distress and mental illness.

Chapter ten provides the research findings and expresses the data collected, along with my clinical recommendations. Additionally, this chapter includes recommendations from Black church parishioners, Black licensed mental health professionals within the Black church, and clergy of the Black church

CHAPTER TWO

How Long Can the Black Church Be Silent?

"Every year, without any treatment at all, thousands stop
suffering from depression. Because it kills them."
—Dr. Paul Greencard

It appears to be common in the twenty-first century for every major platform to discuss suicide except the Black Church. While we do take the time to discuss mental health, the topic most often left out is suicide. Breaking news from TMZ (which stands for "thirty-mile zone"), an American celebrity news website, keeps us abreast of who dies by suicide. Screenwriter and founder of the Shade Room, Angelica Nwandu, updates us on the suicides of celebrities. Leo Flowers, a TEDx speaker and stand-up comedian with a master's in counseling/psychology, created a podcast called *Before You Kill Yourself* to address the topic of suicide.

Furthermore, the hip-hop world excels at creating lyrics—not only to give the topic of suicide a platform but also to express personal suicidal ideations. According to pop culture and music writer Axl Banks, Christopher "Biggie" Wallace's album Ready to Die sold over six million copies.[26] British rapper Dave won the 2020 Brit Award for Album of the Year for his debut studio album Psychodrama. The album delved into his older brother's experiences and the impact of their prison convictions on him, as well as his struggles with mental health and the challenges facing Black working-class youth in Britain.[27]

According to Ben Drodsky, the Arts & Entertainment section editor at Emory University, "When the average American thinks of hip-hop, introspection may not be the image that comes to mind. However, in the past decades of the genre's evolution, artists have become increasingly interested in discussing the hardships that take place inside their minds and bodies in addition to those that occur outside."[28] Many sing and rap about the pain they cannot or aren't ready to talk about. It's no coincidence that rapper Jay-Z wrote, "Never seen it comin' down my eyes, but I gotta make the song cry." In a 2017 interview with New York Times executive editor Dean Baquet, Jay-Z discussed the meaning behind those lyrics. He responded, "The strongest thing a man could do is cry. To expose your feelings, to be vulnerable in front of the world. That's real strength. You know, you feel like you gotta be this guarded person. That's not real. It's fake."[29]

Baquet followed up by asking about the unhappiness Jay-Z might have felt at the time. Jay-Z responded, "Well, you compartmentalize, right? So you can be inside your body and be happy, but at the core of it, something else is going on."[30] Notice for a moment that he used the term "compartmentalize." He hit the nail on the head. This is what the Black church does every Sunday morning: we compartmentalize our suicidal thoughts to look the part while internally falling apart. This is the silence of sabotage at its finest. How can we talk about the death of Christ in church, the death we will all face one day, and read obituaries of those we will see in that "great getting-up morning," but ignore the living who wish they were dead right in our congregations?

THE BIBLICAL LITERATURE

As with every dissertation for one's doctorate, the "lit" review is vital to one's research. During this process, the researcher meticulously examines past studies on the chosen topic. Since this is both theological and psychological research, why not review the oldest manuscript in human history: the Holy Scriptures? The Bible does not shy away from the sensitive topic of suicide. I am a firm Kingdom-minded believer that anything the Bible addresses, the church should also address—especially the Black church.

Interestingly enough, the Bible, which I often refer to as "the Kingdom Document" (because it is a book about the King of kings and the clash between the Kingdom of Christ and the kingdom of darkness), actually records seven narrative accounts of people who committed suicide. While we will discuss these biblical accounts throughout this book, this chapter will focus on the suicide of a man in the Bible named Zimri.

> *15 In the twenty-seventh year of Asa king of Judah, Zimri reigned in Tirzah seven days. The army was encamped near Gibbethon, a Philistine town. 16 When the Israelites in the camp heard that Zimri had plotted against the king and murdered him, they proclaimed Omri, the commander of the army, king over Israel that very day there in the camp. 17 Then Omri and all the Israelites with him withdrew from Gibbethon and laid siege to Tirzah. 18 When Zimri saw that the city was taken, he went into the citadel of the royal palace and set the palace on fire around him. So he died, 19 because of the sins he had committed, doing evil in the eyes of the LORD and following the ways of Jeroboam and committing the same sin Jeroboam had caused Israel to commit. (1 Kings 16:15-19, NIV)*

How do we address the above passage in the twenty-first century? The passage doesn't read too kindly. Zimri was a man with a secret desire to become king. He wanted more than what was afforded to him. He wasn't satisfied with being a commander under King Elah's authority—he also craved more control.

Interestingly, he only reigned as king for seven days. Wow. I call this the "Suicide of Gain." What do I mean by this? Zimri turned his back on King Elah to take his throne, but when he realized his plan wouldn't work out in his favor, he set the palace on fire.

THE SUICIDE OF GAIN

The "suicide of gain" represents those of us who aspire to be all that we can in this life, but lack the patience to wait on Christ our King, who is far better at elevating us. Zimri's suicide serves as a reminder of the danger in seeking to gain the world while forfeiting one's soul. King Jesus asked a pivotal question: "What does it benefit someone to gain the whole world and yet lose their life? What can anyone give in exchange for his life?" (Mark 8:36-37, CSB). Interestingly, this "suicide of gain" has plagued the Black church.

While many of us come looking the part—dressed up, jewelry shining from wide-rimmed hats, high heels, alligator skin shoes, and fancy watches—we carry the pain of not being where we want to be financially, corporately, and socially. Many in the congregation of the Black church are overwhelmed, tired, and mentally at the end of their rope due to not being able to succeed in a racist-dominated world, finding some relief for a few hours on Sunday morning in the pews of the Black church. This chronic feeling among people of color—that we don't measure up and aren't good enough—takes a toll on our mental and physical health.

Licensed marriage and family therapist Natalie Y. Gutierrez can identify with the pain of not having or being enough as a person of color in a white-dominated world, which she refers to as materialism:

> Materialism is the obsession with material wealth and the consumption of physical goods over the nurturing of relationships or real self-care. It tends to come from the implicit belief that visibly having 'more' equates to increased power and worth. As someone of the global majority, you're specifically vulnerable to this cultural legacy burden if you've grown up in poverty, learning that scarcity is scary and threatening. If you're like me, you might find yourself seeking out the instant gratification of things, or ownership of possessions in excess, to try to soothe your painful memories of not having enough.[31]

While many pastors and clergy of color desire to offer help in urban communities, they often lack the necessary resources and finances that white pastors and clergy already have. Make no mistake, the Black church is full of ideas, dreams, and aspirations. However, we are simply lacking the necessary resources and finances. Historian, scholar, and professor Barber D. Savage comments on this dilemma in Black churches during the 2012 economic recession:

Even before the downturn in the economy, the most pressing social issue in Black communities was poverty, especially among children, and continuing inequities in educational and employment opportunities. The recession made a bad situation worse, including among Black middle-class families affected by steep declines in public sector jobs. Many Black churches have seen their own finances plummet along with those of their members. Still, most of those churches continue to offer direct assistance and other services. Some Black religious leaders also advocate on economic and equality issues precisely because they know that the best efforts of churches are insufficient; we need charitable public policies.[32]

Consequently, the congregants in the pews of the Black church aren't getting the financial assistance they need from clergy and pastors due to the lack of resources. I once heard Reverend Jesse Jackson state, "Poverty is bad for your health." When he made this statement, he was addressing the state of the Black church.

Thus, one cannot discuss suicide in the Black church without addressing the desire for gain. There is nothing wrong with economic growth in the Black church, but the chief complaint of congregants is the perception that the pastor is often the wealthiest person in the building. I once heard a congregant say, "If the preacher is the only one in the Black church with a Bentley, that's a problem for me." This statement reflects a deeper concern—that the pulpit is not addressing the economic struggles of the pews. One might ask, "What does this have to do with suicide among Kingdom believers in the Black church?"

Remember, Reverend Jesse Jackson remarked, "Poverty is bad for your health." Professor of religion and African American studies, Dr. Eddie S. Glaude, Jr., postulates:

> We see its influence spreading, nationally and internationally, as televangelists and celebrity ministers with their megachurches preach its basic tenets. In Black America, this theology overtakes calls for economic empowerment. Freedom dreams are supplanted by the aspiration to wealth, a theology that suits a vision of capitalism that is devastating our communities and country. This gospel of wealth blunts criticism of durable inequality, precisely because wealth and the aspiration for upward mobility are tied to individual spiritual considerations.

Wealth and poverty constitute evidence of God's blessing or punishment. Conspicuous consumption becomes a critical part of the work of faith. Here, Christians are 'blessed entrepreneurs and consumers.'[32]

There are many faithful churchgoers in the Black church who give regularly but silently feel that wealthy Black pastors and churches aren't giving back to them. Glaude argues that the gospel of wealth preached in mega Black churches makes those who can't afford "the good life" feel as if they are being punished by God. However, when one considers the Holy Scriptures, Christ and His apostles saw the poor as just as valuable to Christ their King as the rich.

> *My brothers and sisters, do not show favoritism as you hold on to the faith in our glorious Lord Jesus Christ. 2 For if someone comes into your meeting wearing a gold ring and dressed in fine clothes, and a poor person dressed in filthy clothes also comes in, 3 if you look with favor on the one wearing the fine clothes and say, "Sit here in a good place," and yet you say to the poor person, "Stand over there," or "Sit here on the floor by my footstool," 4 haven't you made distinctions among yourselves and become judges with evil thoughts?5 Listen, my dear brothers and sisters: Didn't God choose the poor in this world to be rich in faith and heirs of the kingdom that he has promised to those who love him? (James 2:1-5, CSB)*

Christ was just as concerned with the poor man who didn't have any "good clothes" to wear to church as He was with the rich man who was shown more favor. I ask again, how long can we be silent? The Bible is clear that Christ came to preach the gospel of the Kingdom to the poor (Luke 7:22). Christ gospel was called "This gospel of the Kingdom" (Matthew 24:14), which is why James refers to the poor as *"rich in faith and heirs of the kingdom."* Now let's be clear, all Black churches aren't mega churches, and all mega church Pastors aren't greedy. Nevertheless, one thing is certain, Christ said, *"You always have the poor with you"* (Mark 14:7, CSB).

Poverty & Depression in the Black Church

It is reported that African Americans would have higher levels of depression, given that we are more likely to experience life circumstances (such as poverty) and events (life stressors) that represent risk factors for the development of depression.[34] As a group, African Americans demonstrate high levels of religious involvement, with 90% attending religious services (outside of weddings and funerals), and among attendees, about 70% attend services at least a few times a month.[35] With such high statistics on the level of involvement African Americans have within the Black church, there is also significant financial investment. LiveSteez research shows that Black churches, as of 2013, have collectively received more than $420 billion in tithes and donations since 1980.[36]

However, while the Black church is known for having a higher rate of giving than white congregations,[37] members of the Black church are still living paycheck to paycheck, which adds to the mental health struggle. In many Black churches and organizations/denominations, one wouldn't be able to look at people of color and tell they are facing financial struggles, let alone dealing with suicidal ideations, because we look like wealth. In the African American church, we have become experts at buying what we want with our rent money and purchasing what we need with our credit cards. This is another form of slavery that the Black church knows all too well.

Pastor DeForest Soaries Jr. postulates that there are three types of spending that enslave the Black church: compensatory consumption—spending to gain significance; conspicuous consumption—spending to gain status; and confused consumption—impulsive and just plain foolish spending.[38] This silence surrounding the suicide of gain is killing the Black church and the Black community. While we are "treating ourselves" after taking care of everyone else, we struggle to set boundaries and find ourselves stressed out by the debt of trying to impress each other on Sunday mornings with our flamboyant attire. Soaries further argues:

> You have to admit that you are a slave to debt. If you have mail that you know contains bills and it's three months old, and you refuse to open it because you know what's inside, and there's no need to open a letter asking you for money that you don't have—you have a problem. If you're using a credit card to pay off another credit card, even though they've said you'll pay no interest for now—you have a problem. If you find yourself shopping and waiting until your spouse is not home to sneak in what you bought—first, because you don't want them to know you're spending money, and second, because if they find out, they'll want to spend more money, too—then you both have a problem.[39]

Poverty continues to damage the mental health of the Black church, as many use their credit cards to numb trauma and suicidal ideations. Kingdom scholar, pastor, and theologian Dr. Dana Carson asserts:

Poverty continues to damage the mental health of the Black church, as many use their credit cards to numb trauma and suicidal ideations.

> Poor/poverty is often viewed merely as severe economic or material lack—the psycho-social dimensions are overlooked—so money and

material are thrown at the problem, yet the problem remains. Poverty eradication does not mean every country or community attaining a standard of living where each citizen has a Beverly Hills-style mansion, a three-car garage, a sports car in the driveway, a swimming pool, and a boat. Wealth and poverty are relative... Poor/poverty also includes humiliation, fear, shame, powerlessness, feelings of social isolation, inferiority, voicelessness, hopelessness—and a whole lot more.[40]

In the Black church, we have mastered looking the part while mentally falling apart. We wear our silence like a badge of honor. We give to the church, we give to our families, we give to charities, and we give white supremacists our labor and hard-earned money. Additionally, we burden ourselves with more debt by comforting our wounds with retail therapy. The irony is, many of our brothers and sisters in the Black church know that we are in financial debt but don't want to disrupt our shopping sprees by telling us to get our credit together. Nevertheless, getting our credit checked will reveal that we need our mental health checked as well.

"I HAVE JESUS, BUT I DON'T HAVE INSURANCE"

One of the biggest myths in the church is "Long as I got King Jesus, I don't need nobody else." While that sounds real good and "churchy," it definitely puts our mental health at risk. This is what I call "church learned behaviors." There remains an ignorance in many churches that value lyrics over sound doctrine.

When our gospel songs don't line up with Scripture, we must choose the Word of God first. While many believe they are the church, Christ saw the church as one, namely His bride (1 Corinthians 12:12-13/Ephesians 5:25-27).

The church is not, and never has been, about the individual, but a collective body of Kingdom-minded believers fellowshipping together. In fact, the Word of God commands us, "not abandoning our own meeting together, as is the habit of some people, but encouraging one another; and all the more as you see the day drawing near" (Hebrews 10:25, LSB). Carson states profoundly:

The church is not, and never has been, about the individual, but a collective body of Kingdom-minded believers fellowshipping together.

> Nothing replaces physical gathering and the church's power when it gathers. During times of social, political, and economic crisis, people turn to the church. During the world wars, they turned to the church; during Vietnam, they turned to the church; in past pandemics, they turned to the church; and after the September 11, 2001 attack on America, church attendance increased because people once again turned to the church. The church is the ultimate voice, representing God on earth.[41]

Carson further reminds us that the church could not be labeled as an individual, only as a gathered community. This means the individual is defined by the corporate, not the corporate by the individual. We are a community of individuals, not an individual community.[42] In order for the Black church to remain the pillar of hope for the Black community as it has always been (some may disagree), we must divorce the "Long as I got King Jesus, I don't need nobody else" theology.

Licensed clinical social worker, trauma therapist, and minister Dr. Anita Phillips contends that "the life of Jesus' purpose was consummated in community. By the same token, our individual choice to follow Jesus Christ is only individual for a moment. In the time it takes to say 'Amen,' we become members of a new community, the children of one Father, 'of whom the whole family in heaven and earth is named.'"[43]

The caveat is that the Black church community must network with the mental health community. For decades, people of color believed that "Black people don't do therapy." While this perception has changed significantly over time, there is still bias regarding mental health experts. Going to therapy has been viewed as a sign of weakness and something to be ashamed of.[44] One cannot forget the lasting effects of the famous Tuskegee experiment on African Americans.

According to Aaron E. Carroll, professor of pediatrics at Indiana University, researchers found that after this experiment, which ended in 1972, mistrust among African Americans toward the medical profession peaked.[45] This explains why the Black church should take both physical and mental health seriously and assist their congregants in finding a mental health professional they are comfortable with. It's no secret that people of color were encouraged to accomplish goals they didn't think possible until hearing the preacher remind them that they can do all things through Christ who gives them strength (Philippians 4:13). Now, with student loan debts, disappointing credit scores, and the cost of looking good on Sunday morning to impress each other for a few hours, the question arises: who is going to pay for therapy?

According to journalist Taylor Bryant, the number one barrier to Black mental health today is cost. She states, "Despite the Affordable Care Act, around 12% of African Americans are uninsured." [46] Furthermore, psychologist Dr. LaToya Gaines states, "Even those with health insurance often don't have mental health services covered or have expensive co-pays or deductibles."[47]

Psychologist and author Dr. Jennifer Mullan remarks:

> For many people who do not have access to high-end private practice therapists and coaches, community mental health and non-profit group practices are the go-to for mental health needs. These practices and nonprofits primarily employ recently graduated social work, counseling, and psychology students at the rate of $30-50/hour for a 55-minute session, for which the group practice charges anywhere from $150-200 an hour.[48]

Why is this information regarding early-career clinicians vital to making sure people of color are getting the best care possible? Mullan further explains, "In turn, clients have poor outcomes because there is constant burnout and turnover within the staff. This continues to affect people seeking support and increases feelings of abandonment and mistrust in the system."[49]

It's frustrating for many of our parishioners in the Black church to find insurance for a good therapist, psychologist, or psychiatrist. It's also disappointing that they're not in close proximity to our inner cities, urban communities, and rural areas. Pastor and author Dr. Charles A. Moody, Jr. explains how the system of racism contaminates Black neighborhoods, leading to shorter life expectancies where people of color reside. The Washington Post confirms this through research:

> Blacks and Native Americans predominate in many of the neighborhoods at the bottom of the list and have much shorter life expectancies than people of other races and ethnicities. Poor nutrition, obesity, diabetes, and substance abuse are often listed as contributing factors.[50]

The Washington Post's research findings confirm what the Black church already knows to be true. How long can we be silent about the contributing factors of suicide among Kingdom believers in the Black church? Moody further states:

> Growing up in the right environment and the right neighborhood will automatically impact what school you attend. The school you attend will directly influence the type of healthcare system you can access and the lifestyle you can enjoy.[51]

The plight of the Black church is disappointing. While there are plenty of churches in the Black community, there's a shortage of mental health experts, psychiatrists, and psychologists. We must use what has always been our lifeline: our voice. Gutierrez remarks, "Racism attempts to violate your soul. It interrupts your life, and you might find yourself silencing your voice and numbing out."[52]

While many of us in the Black church, which is made up of the Black community, are trying to keep up appearances, we aren't investing in our mental health as we should. I once heard Bishop T.D. Jakes say:

> It's been said if you give a rich person money, they'll invest it. If you give a middle-class person money, they will pay off all their bills. If you give a poor person money, they'll spend it. You know why? There's a desperate feeling of never having this chance again. So the only chance you think you have is to go down to Macy's and have a big shopping spree so you can look rich. But there's a difference between being rich and looking rich.[53]

Often in the Black church, there is unspoken pain. The loss of hope has us self-medicating our trauma with clothes, jewelry, and other things that make us feel better while not getting to the root of our pain. The story of Zimri, who went after what was not his and died an untimely death, reminds us of the dangers of chasing false hopes. Our youth, too, have become so depressed by poverty that some have resorted to robbery, theft, and worse.

Moody postulates:

> The Harvard study found that children affected by the negative, traumatic experiences of poverty—such as worrying about where they will eat, sleep, and live—experience changes in brain architecture.[54]

Our children need the voice of the Black church. Our Black women need the voice of the Black church. Our incarcerated Black men need the voice of the Black church. Those of us hiding our trauma behind "a praise break" need the voice of the Black church. Our inner cities and urban areas need the voice of the Black church. The Black church needs to be the voice it has always been. While we are obeying the voice of Christ, we are neglecting our mental health due to the shame of giving it a voice. It's not enough for the Black church to sing *Lift Every Voice* if we can't voice thoughts of suicidal ideations.

CHAPTER THREE

Silence Doesn't Treat

"I knew with silence comes pain."
—Kobe Campbell

In 2018, the world was shocked by the suicide of fashion icon Kate Spade. She was found dead in her New York apartment, and the New York Medical Examiner's Office announced that her death was a suicide by hanging.[55] According to her husband, she had been suffering from depression and anxiety and had been under treatment for five years prior to her death.[56] I had never heard of her before her suicide, but I was shocked when I discovered how famous she was in the fashion industry and the wealth she had accumulated. According to writer Vallari Vaidya, Spade's net worth at the time of her death was $2 million.[57]

Additionally, Spade's sister, Reta Saffo, expressed that her sister's suicide was a shock in every way.[58] However, Spade had mentioned in a 2017 interview that she battled anxiety, often feeling like "the sky is falling."[59] Saffo also shared that her sister's suicidal thoughts may have started when news broke of actor Robin Williams' suicide in 2014.[60] I remember hearing about Spade's death, which made me deeply concerned for a woman whose life I hadn't even known about until her suicide was announced on the radio.

Parallels Between Spade and the Black Church

While one may argue that Kate Spade was not a person of color, allow me to make something very clear in this dissertation. As a secular clinician licensed by the state of New Jersey, but also as a licensed Christian marriage and family therapist, I am concerned about the suicide of all races, people, and ethnicities. However, I see some similarities between the events leading up to and surrounding Spade's suicide that are tantamount to issues in the Black church, which I will now divulge.

The most obvious thing about Spade's suicide is that she openly admitted in 2017 that she was struggling with mental health. Often, one's suicide comes as a shock, but the mental health of that person is taken for granted. In the Black community and the Black church, people testify about their mental health without actually testifying about their mental health. In the Black church, there is what we call "Testimony Service." This is the part of the service where one testifies about how good God has been to them all week—what they overcame and what they are still confronting, whether financially, occupationally, relationally, in their families, or with their health.

Growing up in the Black church, one didn't get up and say, "Y'all pray for me. I've been having thoughts of suicide." The topic itself was frowned upon by many in the Black church, who believed that suicide is the quickest way to go to hell. Furthermore, it wouldn't have been taken seriously, as it is today, due to the Black church's mistrust and biases against mental health professionals. However, **people would cover their mental health struggles when they testified with phrases like, "I'm not going to let**

> **People would cover their mental health struggles when they testified with phrases like, "I'm not going to let the devil get me down," "The devil is busy," and "I say hallelujah anyhow."**

the devil get me down," "The devil is busy," and "I say hallelujah anyhow."

Next, we should consider that while Spade knew the art of looking good on the outside, she was struggling to live internally. In the Black church, fashion is definitely a trend in many denominations like the Church of God in Christ (COGIC), Apostolic churches, Baptist, and A.M.E. (African Methodist Episcopal) churches. Fashion is such a big thing in the Black church that many congregants have changed their membership or left the church altogether. One of my friends who left the church over this issue stated, "It always felt like a fashion show." I recall growing up that Mother's Day, Father's Day, and Easter were the three times a year when struggling Black families would spend hundreds of dollars on suits, dresses, hats, and shoes—only to go back to the pastor a few months later for money to pay their rent. Looking better is certainly not a remedy for treating mental health. Spade's life exemplifies this sad reality.

Another parallel between Spade and the Black church is the lack of community. Spade's sister, Reta Saffo, stated that Spade was "surrounded by 'yes' people for far too long," and therefore, she didn't receive the proper care for what Saffo believed to be bipolar disorder, which she tried numerous times to help her sister seek treatment for.[61] **The irony in the Black church is that we are surrounded by people who want us to say yes to Jesus but no to therapy.** Ghanaian-American trauma therapist (LCMHC) and author, Kobe Campbell, comments on this reality:

"It can feel incredibly shameful to say we believe in Jesus and yet are so wounded. Christians are supposed to have unwavering hope, right? When I experienced my first depressive episode as a new and eager Christian, I thought it would be safe to share what I was going through. However, I was told by a leader that my depression was ruining my witness. 'Who would want to follow a Jesus who has depressed followers?' this leader said. I still tear up thinking about that moment—and all the moments of lonely, pain-filled silence that followed it. I vowed to never let anyone see me sad again. If they were disappointed in me, how much more was God? That's trauma."[62]

By the grace of God and therapy, Campbell revoked that view and is now helping millions through her private practice and groundbreaking book *Why Am I Like This: How to Break Cycles, Heal from Trauma, and Restore Your Faith.* Many who struggle with suicidal ideations in the Black church can identify with Campbell. When will the church, particularly the Black church, realize that Christ cares about our minds as well as our bodies and souls (more on this in chapter six)? In fact, there is no translation out of the kingdom of darkness into the Kingdom of Christ without repentance, which is the Greek word metanoeō (met-an-o-eh'-o), meaning to change one's mind for the better, heartily amending with abhorrence of one's past sins.

Lastly, a close source to the family described Spade as a "kind, generous, funny, warm, and extremely private person."[63] This intrigued me as a licensed therapist because this "extremely private" success icon mentioned in 2017 that "the sky is falling," attributing it to her anxiety. Furthermore, she had been separated from her husband for the ten months prior to her death.[64] Saffo stated that she would fly out to New York from California to help Spade get treatment. Unfortunately, Spade feared that hospitalization would hurt her brand and tried to self-medicate with alcohol.[65]

Did you catch that? Spade, like many in the Black church, didn't want her mental health to conflict with her brand. This also gives some clarity as to why she was so private. In this chapter, I will discuss two forms of suicide that are very prevalent in the Black church: what I have coined the "Suicide of Image" and the "Suicide of Privacy". Now, let's take a look at the former by reviewing the Biblical literature.

The Suicide of Image

50 Next Abimelek went to Thebez and besieged it and captured it. 51 Inside the city, however, was a strong tower, to which all the men and women—all the people of the city—had fled. They had locked themselves in and climbed up on the tower roof. 52 Abimelek went to the tower and attacked it. But as he approached the entrance to the tower to set it on fire, 53 a woman dropped an upper millstone on his head and cracked his skull.54 Hurriedly he called to his armor-bearer, "Draw your sword and kill me, so that they can't say, 'A woman killed him.'" So his servant ran him through, and he died. 55 When the Israelites saw that Abimelek was dead, they went home. (Judges 9:50-55, NIV)

In the above passage, Abimelek was not looking to die, nor was he trying to find a reason to die. However, after realizing a stone had cracked his skull, and that a woman had done it, he was ready to end his life. He was not depressed or struggling with anxiety; he simply wanted to die rather than have his ego bruised. One of the things that is killing the Black community, as well as the Black church, is the need to protect our image. There is a phrase among Black men coined, "Cool." While other ethnicities use this phrase, it takes on a life of its own among Black men:

We'll be the first to remind you it's not easy being a Black man in America; it never has been. If we seem hard on our brothers, it is easy because we know how hard they will have to work to regain control of their destinies. Over time, we admit, we have had to adapt in unique ways to survive, to maintain our sanity, and to excel in areas that were open to us. One important way Black men have tried to

maintain their dignity and keep control of
their anger is by being 'cool.' Even successful
Black athletes have had to work at being cool
in provocative situations as a way to save their
jobs—or even their lives.[66]

Playing it cool may be good for one's image, but it torments the soul. Coolness can shut down other emotional reactions and shield us from our true feelings.[67] Furthermore, what is cool without the "bling" to go with it? According to a business journal published by the Wharton School of the University of Pennsylvania:

> To examine spending by racial groups, Roussanov and his colleagues studied data collected from 1986 to 2002 for the Consumer Expenditure Survey conducted by the Federal Bureau of Labor Statistics. Black and Hispanic households spend up to 30% more than white households of comparable income on visible goods like clothing, cars, and jewelry, the researchers found. This meant that, compared to white households of similar income, the typical Black and Hispanic household spent $2,300 more per year on visible items.[68]

Furthermore, we cannot overlook the gang image in the Black community. Violence, guns, and sex blend well with the coolness of the culture that recruits our young Black males and females through social media and television. Violence is glorified among our Black youth. The interesting fact is that not everyone carries guns with the intention of killing; it's more about the image. Licensed clinical social worker and founder of the Stay Strong Foundation, Terri M. Williams, who is dedicated to youth and mental health advocacy and mentoring, states:

So many young men are picked up for gun possession, but if we look at what happened with Jiwe, we can see that they are not always carrying with the intent to commit violence. Sometimes—maybe often—carrying a gun is a response to the fear of violence. Don't get me wrong, guns are not the answer to anything! But too often, men are punished for responding to their emotional fears in any language except violence.[69]

The suicide of image is all about the lost self-esteem of the Black church that has settled for looking free rather than truly being made whole by the King of Kings.

The suicide of image is killing our young Black men and women softly. Many of our Black women of color have been hurt deeply by absent fathers, fathers who stayed and cheated on their mothers while providing them hush money, enduring domestic violence, rape, molestation, and racial discrimination on many levels. As a result, many have solely focused on "Securing the Bag," being a "Diva," and even becoming so independent that they have forgotten to let King Jesus inside the Pandora's box of their hearts. This is the suicide of image.

The suicide of image cares more about looking happy than about holding on to what Christ has promised them. It has many living to prove a public point while suffering a private pain. The suicide of image has led many of our young adolescent Black men to shoot each other over a pair of sneakers, not realizing (or not caring) that Black males face a higher prison sentence than whites. Licensed clinical social worker, author, and theologian, Dr. Pamela Robinson, argues:

> Current research supports that African Americans are overrepresented on almost every criminal justice statistic. Several studies indicate that there are racial biases in the punishment for at least some crimes. Before the Civil War, laws in the United States explicitly provided for more severe punishment for Blacks than for Whites who were guilty of the same crime. Such legal statutes no longer exist, yet the administration of justice is still especially harsh to Blacks when the victim is white. There is overwhelming evidence that the criminal justice system is racist.[70]

As stated earlier, I am a strong advocate for teaching people the importance of healthy self-worth. I call it "Christ Confident." One of the signs that insecurity is at its apex among any people is when we are using our externals to heal our internals. Getting our hair done is not therapy. Buying clothes we can't afford is not therapy. Using filters on our next social media selfie is not therapy. By the same token, this is what the Black church must understand.

Praise and worship is therapeutic, but we have to watch what we eat. Contributing to the offering is good, but we have to invest in copays to keep up with our doctor's appointments. **Giving God praise as the choir sings is great, but singing the blues on Sunday night and refusing to see a therapist is not good for the soul.** When the Black church takes mental health as seriously as we take our fried chicken dinners, plays, fashion shows, and auxiliaries we are part of, we will see progress in our mental health.

THE SUICIDE OF PRIVACY

The Black church has a code among us where we don't talk about certain things. Most of the ways the Black church treats mental health are reminiscent of the traditional ways Black families operated at home. One of the unwritten rules in Black families is the philosophy of "What goes on in this house, stays in this house." If one thing is certain, most Black families made sure their fidelity was to this philosophy rather than to the Word of God. However, we cannot vilify Black families for taking pride in "being private." This code of privacy that we live by has its roots in chattel slavery.

Dr. Monica McGoldrick and Professor Elaine Pinderhughes postulate that "in the African American community, there is a theme of pain and hurt that is often hidden behind family secrets. These family secrets are deeply rooted in the African American experience of slavery and racism that is carried throughout generations."[71] The insurmountable number of secrets running rampant in the Black community and the church has created an ample amount of shame. Mullan argues that "it is essential to acknowledge, set boundaries, honor, and excavate the root of the shame. As we know, unexamined shame leads to the perpetuation of violence, as we have seen in the Civil Rights Era and beyond."[72]

Gutierrez reminds us that "shame creates disconnection in relationships and completely interferes with your own self-love."[73] Abimelek shows us the link between the suicide of image and the suicide of privacy. Clearly, they are intertwined. He did not want anyone to know that he was killed by a woman, so he made sure a man killed him. Not wanting people to know a woman wounded him was the secret he did not want to get out, and having a man do it to protect his image still killed him.

The suicide of privacy is very prevalent in the Black church. From the censored testimonies in the Black church (where we pick what we want to testify about to appear to be strong soldiers for the Lord Jesus) to the surface-level conversations before and after service—all in the name of "dignity." The suicide of image and privacy creates a special kind of loneliness right in the house of God. While we feel the presence of God, we secretly feel disconnected from our sisters and brothers due to the shame of our unresolved and unspoken mental health.

Pastor Philippe Matthews remarks:

> One of the problems with the disease of depression is that it makes you think that you are the only one going through it, which kills your support system and can subsequently kill you. I suffered from depression since I was a little child, but you didn't know it. Unfortunately, like so many in the Black community, my family was in denial, and I wasn't diagnosed until I was an adult. I was working as a journalist and happened to interview a psychiatrist who authored a book on depression. It was then I realized I had all the symptoms of mild to severe depression.[74]

Interestingly enough, Scripture reminds us that pride comes before a fall (Proverbs 16:18). The pride of trying to "fake it till we make it" is destroying our sanity, increasing depression, and fueling our anxiety. Bishop T. D. Jakes states, "Pride is dangerous because it forces you to lie needlessly in a helpless state for days—and sometimes years."[75] In order for the Black church to address suicide, which shouldn't be a taboo topic, we must be cognizant of the truth that we don't have to be strong all the time.

Is Being Strong Killing Us?

The Black community prides itself on being "strong." From childhood to the nursing home, being strong is what we live by. However, being strong has led many in the Black church to feel more depressed, anxious, ashamed, and guilty for feeling weak. At home, we learned we have to be strong to survive in a white-dominated society. Then we come to church and are told to be strong. Let's be clear: congregants in the Black church don't mind being told to be strong in the Lord, but we mind when you say that being tired is a sin.

One of the popular gospel songs in the Black church is "I've Been Running for Jesus a Long Time; I'm Not Tired Yet." As quietly as it's kept, songs like this in the Black church are not biblical and contribute to the mental health struggles of people of color. When one revisits the biblical accounts, it's evident that there were countless Kingdom believers who got tired. The apostle Paul wrote that he was "despaired of life" (2 Corinthians 1:8); John the Baptizer grew restless while incarcerated (Luke 7:18-23); Jesus Christ, our King, got tired and sat on Jacob's well (John 4:4). Thankfully, the Bible does not condemn the Black church for being tired but promises that Yahweh "gives power to the faint, and to him who has no might He increases strength" (Isaiah 40:29, ESV).

The Black church must realize that trying to be strong 24/7 causes hypertension, cardiovascular issues, displaced anger, depression, restlessness, and silent frustration.

The Black church must realize that trying to be strong 24/7 causes hypertension, cardiovascular issues, displaced anger, depression, restlessness, and silent frustration. Dr. Walker argues:

Resilience in the face of adversity is a strength and a weakness for Black people. Somewhere along the way, we learned that we can never be vulnerable. If someone seems to be suicidal, in any of the ways I have described, it does not mean that you have to 'call them out' for what you see. You can be present and remind them that someone cares. Do for them what you would want someone to do for you when you are down or feeling like life is not worth living. Standing without judgment for someone who needs support is a strength.[76]

Our Black males are stressed, battling hypertension, dying at early ages, and trying to be the breadwinners while navigating a society that will incarcerate a Black male before hiring him. Contrary to popular belief, many of our Black males are genuinely trying to be good husbands and fathers while also being productive in their businesses and places of employment. Even successful men of color live with what I call the "anxiety of white reality"; white men don't have to think twice about just going to work in the morning.

Dr. Mary-Frances Winters highlights the anxiety of Black males in the workplace:

> There are numerous stories of professional Black men who say that even if they are going into the office on a weekend, they dress in business attire for fear of being questioned by security. Even on 'casual Fridays,' Black men often are still very mindful of how their 'look' may trigger negative stereotypes and are more apt to dress more formally—and definitely not wear a hoodie. Hillary Clinton declared in a campaign speech in 2015 that even 'open-minded white people' are sometimes afraid of

hoodie-wearing Black men. Black men often work hard to avoid stereotype threats. This extra emotional labor of constantly wondering whether you look threatening is fatiguing.[77]

This is why the Black church must be a place that takes our Black males in and brings them back to a state of peace and tranquility. African American scholar, Harvard University professor, filmmaker, and author Dr. Henry Louis Gates, Jr. defines the Black church as more than a house of worship but as a "key refuge for many in hard times."[78] Thus, the Black church must remind Black males that it's a place where being weak is not a crime. The Black church must remind our Black males that it is where the strong bear the infirmities of the weak (Romans 15:1). The Bible confirms that even "the youth grow tired and weary, and young men stumble and fall; but those who hope in the LORD will renew their strength" (Isaiah 40:30-31, NIV).

Contrary to popular belief, not all Black men are gangbanging, killing each other, robbing banks, or selling/doing drugs. Dr. Gates, who is an accomplished Harvard University professor and filmmaker with a reported net worth of one million,[79] felt the discrimination and racial profiling that poverty-stricken Black males on minimum wage experience. On July 16, 2009, Gates was arrested in front of his house while trying to get into his front door, which was jammed. After forcing the door open with the help of his cab driver, Sgt. James Crowley of the Cambridge Police Department showed up at his door and asked him to step outside.[80]

Despite the fact that Gates lived there and showed the officer identification, the officer did not believe that a Black male, who was extremely successful, could live there. The officer refused to show Gates his badge number. However, Sgt. Crowley reported that a white female caller notified the police at around 12:45 PM about seeing two Black men on the porch of the home.[81] Nevertheless, Gates was reported for being arrested for yelling at the White officer.[82] Dr. S. Allen Counter, a Black professor at

Harvard Medical School, stated he and a number of his university colleagues were "deeply disturbed about the actions of the Cambridge police."[83] We are tired. Black men struggle even at the height of their careers and success.

Our Black women, who make up a large percentage of the Black church, are also tired of being strong. Tiffany Thomas, pastor of South Tryon Community Church in Charlotte, North Carolina, remarks:

"Black women have a long, intricate history with the church. Women, making up 70 to 90 percent of Black congregations, have always found the institution of the church a place of solace and hope. As far back as African American history begins, during a time when their bodies were bound by the violence of slavery, Black women gathered to worship communally a God who gave freedom and liberation into the salvific power of Christ.[84]

One cannot deny that our Black women are just as stigmatized as our Black males. Being a strong "Black woman" in America carries its own set of challenges. However, what do we say to Black mothers in the Black church whose prayer requests go beyond praying for their health, career advancement, or their homes? Black mothers are praying that their sons get home safely, without facing police brutality or other injustices in this world. African American studies professor Dr. Sheri Parks postulates:

> What were women whose sons had been killed supposed to do? They were supposed to smile, always smile, because the image says that anger is the Black female default emotion, and anytime a Black woman is not smiling, she must be angry. The only negative emotion he could imagine for them, even in grief, was anger. And anger meant dangerous. It explains why the smiling Mammy was important; her smile was a disarmament, a signal that the Black female was safe.[85]

One can see why the Black woman feels safe in the Black church, expressing vibrant emotions of joy, grief, pain, sorrow, and sadness that are easily judged elsewhere. However, the thoughts of Black women that are often left out are those related to suicidal ideations. In a new study emphasizing only women, researchers from Boston University Chobanian & Avedisian School of Medicine and Howard University have linked Black women ages 18–65 to the highest risk for suicide, irrespective of their socioeconomic status.[86] Once again, our silence in the Black church about these issues is troubling.

Furthermore, the findings of the above study indicate that Black women in the highest income bracket had a 20% increase in the odds of suicide or self-inflicted injury compared to white women in the lowest socioeconomic bracket.[87] Clinical instructor of psychiatry at the school, Temitope Ogundare, states, "Our findings were surprising because most studies usually show that the rate of suicide was higher in white women in the U.S. However, when we begin to look at the intersection of race and income, a different picture begins to emerge."[88]

> **Being a "strong Black woman" can lead to untreated mental health issues and even suicide.**

Being a "strong Black woman" can lead to untreated mental health issues and even suicide. However, the deaths of many of our strong Black women in and outside the Black church are not always the result of suicide. Domestic violence and strong Black women don't mix. Parks argues:

> Black women are supposed to be stoic in much the same way that men are traditionally supposed to be stoic, and for precisely the same reasons: If we break down, it is a strong signal that something is very, very wrong. Stoicism can be taken to extremes, as when Black women 'allow' men to beat them so the men can feel

like men at the expense of the women's bodies. The data is mixed about whether women are more or less likely to experience domestic violence—self-reporting is often unwieldy—but when they do, they are more likely to die from it because Black women fight back.[89]

Many of our strong Black women are so committed to being strong that their mental health is put at risk. Additionally, hiding their success poses another mental health risk for women of color. Parks goes on to say:

> Often, Black women are particularly reluctant to talk to men about their success. In a discussion I conducted with Black female graduate students, the women said that they routinely disguised that they were in PhD programs because it made Black men uncomfortable. One woman said, 'I want to have a date.' Some admitted that they have considered leaving graduate school because of the reactions of some Black men.[90]

Domestic violence among Black women is a common tragedy. Parks remarks, "When it was widely reported that singer Chris Brown had beaten his fellow artist and girlfriend, Rihanna, a young Black woman told National Public Radio that 'it happens all the time.'"[91] One can only imagine how much the suicide of image and privacy is affecting our Black men and women. Parks continues:

Black women handle stress differently than men or white women. Men tend to battle the source of the stress. White women are more likely to 'tend and befriend.' Black women are likely to 'tend, befriend, mend, and keep it in.' They double up on roles—caregiver and fixer. This role requires a sort of silence about what they've seen, about whom they've helped, or even about how they feel. But we hold it in, suck it up, and go on.[92]

Often, by the time our Black men and women speak up, two things happen: we are made to feel guilty or misunderstood.

Author, actress, poet, and civil rights activist Dr. Maya Angelou silenced her voice after she told her brother about how her mother's boyfriend raped her. Maya felt guilty for voicing what happened to her, thinking her voice had killed him. Just like Maya Angelou, many of our Black women have stopped talking, as have many of our Black men. One would be amazed at how long guilt, shame, and being misunderstood have silenced the Black church and community.

On the other hand, due to the flamboyant style of dress, colorful music of Black culture, and expression, people of color are often seen as wanting attention. What one fails to realize is that the one looking for attention may be on the verge of suicide. Dr. Walker postulates:

Those of us who are professionally responsible for evaluating suicide risk have language to articulate circumstances for less or more severe risk. Perhaps because this type of language rarely gets to the public, you are less likely to know if your niece's thoughts of suicide are a 'cry for help' or if she really needs help. Speaking of which, it is never okay to say this about someone, as it is dismissive. If someone is doing something to get attention, it would seem that they are in need. They may not be in crisis, but they are nevertheless seeking something that they do not have. You do not want to wait until they are in crisis.[93]

The Black church has spoken loudly about our rights. We have turned up the volume on poverty. We have sounded the alarm on the discrimination against our women. We have made Facebook posts about the salaries of people of color versus whites in the same careers with the same educational requirements. We march when injustices are done to us. We are becoming more comfortable singing, rapping, writing poetry, and publishing books about our mental health. However, the neglected components of mental health and emotional distress, particularly suicide, are the silent killers in the Black church. Until we address this topic, we truly won't understand the congregants we minister to on a weekly basis.

CHAPTER FOUR

Sometimes Saints Just Don't Understand

"Everything is not the devil."
—Anonymous

Till this day, there appears to be a divide between the mental health of the Black church and its theology. While the Black church has accomplished a lot during the civil rights movement and continues to do so, we remain divided on our theology of psychology. Pastor Kenya Proctor, pastor of Ambassadors for Christ Worship Center, lost her close friend years ago. However, she reported finding it hard to talk about it. Religion News Service explains why she couldn't: "Raised in the Black church tradition in Louisiana, Proctor has learned that part of her discomfort in talking about Jay's death has to do with her upbringing; as a clergyperson, she knows that Black pastors are among those who most need to talk about suicide."[94]

Thankfully, Proctor is part of a national movement at the American Foundation for Suicide Prevention, which works with community-based organizations and mental health advocates to train Christian faith leaders on how to talk to their parishes about suicide in the Black community and the Black church.[95] While some clergy are discussing suicide, a vast majority have not. According to the Christian Recorder:

In 2020, suicide was the leading cause of death for Black girls aged 12 to 14. In a May 2022 Forbes Magazine article, 'Why Are More Black Americans Committing Suicide?' author Maia Niguel Hoskin references unrecognized depression as a contributing cause of these suicides. Additionally, the Centers for Behavioral Health Statistics and Quality have found that despite a 2020 rate decrease overall, there is an increase in Black suicide.[96]

The question is: how do we deal with these issues when they are covered in the silence of "I'm blessed and highly favored?" How can the Black church, which has been such a staple in the Black community, be the last place where one would discuss suicidal ideations? According to licensed trauma psychologist Dr. La Keita D. Carter:

In the Black church, the pastor isn't just invited to family weddings because they will marry folks and do funerals because they will eulogize folks. We invite our pastors to graduation parties, baby showers, house blessings, retirement parties, and birthday parties. And they do their best to oblige. Our pastors are our extended families, which is why it's so easy for us to go to them when life throws us curveballs, as opposed to trained professionals. It's an easy choice to make when you have a problem: go to the trusted, extended family member who has a history of being supportive rather than a perfect stranger.[97]

Thus, one can see why this research is being conducted. The Black church isn't just a place where we go to worship; it's an extended family. However, if one cannot discuss their true emotions, suicidal ideations, and past attempts, then the Black church becomes a family with too many secrets. We are already hiding from White America, but we are also hiding from each other.

Because the pastor is often looked to for counseling, it's crucial that clergy are educated in mental health. If clergy only offer prayer and Scriptures for mental health issues—especially suicidal ideations—without referrals to licensed therapists or psychologists, the Black community's suicide rates may continue to increase. This does not mean that God is not able; it simply means we aren't educated and trained on suicidality.

When congregants tell clergy in the Black church about their physical health issues, like hypertension, cholesterol, diabetes, and other ailments, the pastor encourages them to "go get that checked" after or before praying for them. Why isn't our mental health, which can cause issues with our physical health, taken just as seriously? Consequently, if clergy have biases against psychological training, it may be best to leave the mental health aspect to licensed professionals. Carter further argues:

> The pastor's lane is spiritual guidance and support. It is not psychology, which is the study of the human mind and behavior. And it's not mental health treatment, which is the application of scientific techniques and interventions to treat emotional and psychiatric problems. It's certainly acceptable to ask the pastor for prayer, and sometimes they may even have professional referrals to offer. However, to expect your pastor to provide treatment or consultation about mental health concerns would be

like expecting them to perform heart surgery
on you or diagnose your ear infection.[98]

While the above statement is highly accurate, there are clergy in the Black church who believe in therapy and are therapists themselves. In fact, psychologist Dr. Thema Bryant was the 2023 president of the American Psychological Association (APA), the largest organization with more than 130,000 members.[99] Bryant is also a tenured professor at Pepperdine University and an ordained elder in the African Methodist Episcopal Church (AME). Dr. Bryant was honored by the Institute of Violence, Abuse and Trauma with a media award for the film Psychology of Human Trafficking in 2016. Thankfully, Dr. Bryant directs the mental health ministry at First AME Church in South Los Angeles.

Dr. Bryant is one of many clergy who are clinical psychologists and who understand the plight of mental health in the Black church. While there have been Black psychologists, clinicians, and therapists around for decades, many of them were not clergy. The Black Psychiatrist of America was founded in 1969 to address the needs of minorities that traditional government and professional organizations were not responsive to regarding the ever-evolving priorities of the African American community and their mental health needs.[100] They challenged the APA, which is astonishing, considering that Dr. Bryant became the fourth Black woman to be president in 2023.[101]

Dr. Bryant overcame sexual trauma and published her groundbreaking book, *Homecoming: Overcome Fear and Trauma to Reclaim Your Whole, Authentic Self.* She states:

> There's a difference between stress and
> traumatic stress. All of us have day-to-day
> stress or strain; you have a lot of responsibil-
> ities, or people can annoy you or irritate you.
> But when we talk about trauma, it is those
> experiences that overwhelm my usual capacity

to cope, that actually disrupt my nervous system. So, if I'm upset with you today and feel
better tomorrow, that wasn't trauma.[102]

UNHEALED HEALERS

If Black clergy in the Black church are skeptical about the topic of mental health and suicidality, it may also reveal that their own mental health hasn't been addressed. According to lead researcher Dan Bolger:

> Pastors are feeling overwhelmed because the need in Black communities often exceeds their abilities. Church members were often open to seeing a mental health professional, but only if they were referred by their pastor. Congregants told us that they would seek their pastor first because they perceived mental health issues as highly stigmatized, not only in their church but also in the broader community, and they saw their pastor as uniquely qualified to help address such concerns.

Maybe Black clergy's reluctance to discuss mental health could be attributed to reasons beyond thinking suicide is a taboo topic; they could be hiding from their own suicidal ideations. In 2013, 42-year-old Pastor Teddy Parker Jr., pastor of Bibb Mount Zion Baptist Church in Macon, Georgia, put a gun to his head after sending his wife off to church. His friend, Dr. E. Dewey Smith, admitted that Pastor Parker was suffering from manic depression and had been facing emotional issues but "couldn't back away from ministry."[105]

It is pivotal that clergy in the Black church understand the importance of self-care and balance in order to assist their parishioners with their mental health. During the COVID-19 pandemic, a study surveying 218 Black clergy revealed that Black pastors identified their most challenging stressors as member dynamics, financial stress, leading a church to fulfill its mission, and the pastor's workload.[106] The survey also revealed that 72.5% of Black pastors reported moderate to extreme stress levels, and 77% acknowledged experiencing moderate to extreme stress levels during social protests for the deaths of Black people at the hands of law enforcement.[107]

It's hard to assist parishioners in coming out of denial while we are in denial about the frequency, intensity, and duration of our mental health struggles as clergy in the Kingdom of Christ. It is vital to understand that while the Black church is silent about our mental health and suicidality, it does not prohibit our mental illness, emotional distress, and suicidality from manifesting in bodily expressions, self-destructive behaviors, and self-sabotaging actions.

> It's hard to assist parishioners in coming out of denial while we are in denial about the frequency, intensity, and duration of our mental health struggles as clergy in the Kingdom of Christ.

> According to the National Study of American Life, "Though whites experience depression more often, African Americans and Caribbean Blacks experience greater severity and persistence.

THE SIGNS OF SILENCE

While this dissertation is in no way intended to minimize mental health and suicidality among whites, the objective is to educate the world at large about the mental health, emotional distress, and suicidality of people of color. **According to the National Study of American Life, "Though whites experience depression more often, African**

Americans and Caribbean Blacks experience greater severity and persistence. Depression is more disabling for African Americans and takes a greater toll on all aspects of life—including work, relationships, social, and overall—than non-whites."[108]

Dr. Bryant argues, "Survival for Black people in America has necessitated the mastery of masking emotions of discontent in particular."[109] Thus, we must understand what depression, anxiety, emotional distress, and suicidality, among many others, look like in the Black church and Black community. Williams outlines the manifestations of depression in people of color:

> Depression looks like your cousin who just got sentenced for dealing four grams of cocaine. It looks like your sister who works eighteen-hour days and hasn't made it to Sunday dinner in weeks. Depression looks like your sixteen-year-old neighbor who's having her second baby. Depression looks like the boy whose drive-by shot hit your niece instead of the rival gang member he was gunning for. Depression looks like the black-and-blue bruise on your troubled nephew's wife. Depression is the overweight mother of two who keeps forgetting to take her blood pressure medicine and has a heart attack in the supermarket where you shop every week. Depression looks like the corporate executive who wears an airtight game face all day and collapses at home every night, so tired of acting the part that he can't enjoy his own life.[110]

This is what I call the signs of silence. These manifestations are not taken seriously due to the fact that some of the above examples clearly demonstrate Black people who are on the go, busy trying to balance family and life. Most of all, we are suffering in silence and dying in public due to private mental health struggles and untreated emotional distress. Williams continues:

> Depression looks like the twenty-eight-year-old Black woman who's starving herself to death to look like white models in her industry. Depression looks like your pastor who preaches like a man lit up with the Holy Spirit on Sunday mornings and drinks himself to sleep every night. Depression looks like your best friend who's stopped cleaning her house or doing her hair or taking any interest in your friendship. Depression is the co-worker who's chronically late and blames everyone else for her missed promotions. Depression is your uncle's suicide that no one wants to talk about. And, yes, depression is being angry and irritable every day for months on end.[111]

Why is it vital to understand the manifestations of depression in the Black church and within the Black community? Williams explains, "Suicide is the most obvious way that depression kills, and according to statistics, five African Americans a day take their own lives. But as frightening as those numbers are, they represent only a fraction of the deaths that can be laid at depression's doorstep."[112]

SUCCEEDING WHILE BLACK

If one thinks that individuals in the Black community and the Black church are finished with mental health and suicidality after becoming successful, we are sadly mistaken. Suicidal thoughts don't just follow Black men to the alley, the homeless Black individual to an abandoned building, or the overworked Black woman to a locked bathroom door. Suicidal thoughts prompted Christopher "Biggie Smalls" Wallace to rap, "Suicidal; I'm ready to die." Suicidal thoughts followed Kansas City Chiefs linebacker Jovan Belcher, who shot himself after shooting his girlfriend. Clinical psychologist Dr. Paul A. Hauck postulates, "When a famous person attempts or succeeds at suicide, the suicide rate in the nation takes a big jump."[114]

> **Success while Black doesn't take away mental health issues.**

Success while Black doesn't take away mental health issues. In 1973, soulful singer Donnie Hathaway wrote a powerful song, "Take it from me, someday we'll all be free." He wrote to inspire people of color enduring racism, poverty in urban areas, and struggling homes to remember that we must not give up on freedom and social justice. However, in 1979, Donnie Hathaway died after falling from the 15th floor of his Essex House room at 160 Central Park South.[115] Hathaway battled mental health challenges, diagnosed as a paranoid schizophrenic. Schizophrenia involves a range of problems with thinking (cognition), behavior, and emotions. Signs and symptoms may vary but usually involve delusions, hallucinations, or disorganized speech, reflecting an impaired ability to function.[116]

While it is still speculated today about the cause of his fall from that fifteen-story hotel, it does not dismiss the evidence-based fact that the leading cause of death among those diagnosed with schizophrenia is suicide.[117] Clearly, success did not erase the mental health struggles of this Black man, whose music is still played today, and a play was done in his honor during mental health awareness month. The Black Church must be concerned. Donnie Hathaway grew up in the Black Church, singing and playing the piano.[118]

On June 30, 1995, soulful singer Phyllis Hyman was scheduled to sing at the Apollo in New York. However, she had not come out of her room for hours. Tragically, Hyman was found dead after taking a lethal mix of pills and alcohol, alone in her apartment.[119] Hyman had been diagnosed with bipolar disorder, previously known as manic depression.[120] Bipolar disorder is a chronic mood disorder that causes intense shifts in mood, energy levels, and behavior. Manic and hypomanic episodes are the main signs of the condition, and most people with bipolar disorder also experience depressive episodes. The condition is manageable with medications, talk therapy, lifestyle changes, and other treatments.[121]

While she was called the "Diva," Phyllis's self-worth was gone. Although she was clinically diagnosed, Hyman refused to take her medicine, self-medicating through overeating and alcohol addiction.[122] While Hyman was a strong advocate for AIDS awareness, she was tired of fighting and self-medicating. Clearly, success does not heal the trauma of pain among the Black community and the Black church. The common trait that Hathaway and Hyman had in common was their refusal to take medication. This is also common in the Black church: self-medicating our trauma. While we know Jesus is in the house, the question one must ask is, is there a mental health expert in the house of the Black church?

Often, successful Black clergy are seen as celebrities and are envied and mimicked by storefront churches. However, having a megachurch does not exempt one from suicidality. According to *Time Magazine*, Pastor Jarrid Wilson, who frequently spoke out on mental health issues and his own struggles with depression, died by suicide.[123] While this white pastor made major headlines after his death, the suicides in the Black church among clergy and parishioners are not reported as much due to the privacy surrounding suicide, as discussed in Chapter Three.

Giving The Silent Killer
the Silent Treatment

When the mental health of the Black church is not addressed, it manifests in self-destruction. Williams reports, "To look at the life-threatening effects and side effects of depression when it's not acknowledged: suicide, crime, addiction, overeating, high blood pressure, overwork, juvenile detention, prison relapse, sexually transmitted diseases, shattered relationships, job loss, hopelessness."[124] We will discuss this in greater detail in the next chapter. In the meantime, the question arises: what causes the Black church and the Black community to remain silent about their mental health? This goes deeper than just stigma, shame, and fear. It is also what I call the suicide of unmet expectations.

Let's go back to the Bible and look at the suicide of Judas:

> *3 Then when Judas, his betrayer, saw that Jesus was condemned, he changed his mind and brought back the thirty pieces of silver to the chief priests and the elders, 4 saying, "I have sinned by betraying innocent blood." They said, "What is that to us? See to it yourself." 5 And throwing down the pieces of silver into the temple, he departed, and he went and hanged himself. (Matthew 27:3-5, ESV)*

Judas was one of the original twelve disciples that King Jesus picked. He was also the treasurer of the group (John 13:29). He was there when Christ fed multitudes, walked on water, cast out demons, and raised the dead. The question is, how could one of Jesus Christ's disciples hang himself? Judas, like many other Jews, had the expectation that the Kingly Messiah would come and set up a political kingdom to overthrow their enemies, namely, the Romans. This is the kind of King Judas wanted in Jesus.

In Christ's day, there was a group of Jews known as the Zealots. Dr. Carson states, "Regarding God alone as their sovereign, they attempted to overthrow the Romans and those who collaborated with them by violent means, including assassination. They helped to incite and encourage the Jewish revolt of 66-73 AD."[125] However, Christ made it clear that His Kingdom was not of this world (John 18:36). When Judas betrayed Jesus for thirty pieces of silver in the garden of Gethsemane, King Jesus made it clear to the authorities that came to arrest Him, "Do you think that I cannot appeal to my Father, and he will at once send me more than twelve legions of angels?" (Matthew 26:53, ESV). Judas betrayed Jesus due to unmet expectations that Christ would overthrow the Romans. What Judas was not cognizant of is that Christ came to overthrow the works of Satan (1 John 3:8).

Racism against Jews was common in the first century, which is why the concept of the coming Messiah meant everything to them. Judas, being a Jew, was upset that what he expected Christ to do as the Kingly Messiah was not done. There are many in the Black church who sit in the pews week after week, carrying historical trauma and the pains of racism in their hearts. Dr. Eric Mason argues:

> *Every twenty or thirty years, Blacks become newly aware that America is a strange land. Racism and injustice reawaken us to the reality that the tears in the fabric of the American story are still ripping, as they have been since 1619 when slaves first arrived at Jamestown. From Emmett Till to Rodney King to Hurricane Katrina to Michael Brown to George Floyd, each scenario reawakens in African Americans a profound awareness that things haven't changed a bit. When this happens, Christianity is recognized to be a tool that has often been utilized to perpetuate injustice towards Blacks.[126]*

While the Black church is still trying to heal from over 400 years of chattel slavery, we are constantly re-traumatized by systematic racism that manifests in police brutality, denied opportunities, and unfair pay despite the fact that we

have the same educational background and skills as our white counterparts. Consequently, this produces and adds to the historical trauma of the Black church, which relies on clergy on Sunday mornings for a Word from the King of kings. Dr. Martin Luther King, Jr., remarked, as he reflected on the injustices faced by people of color while confined to a prison cell, fighting for civil rights:

> While the Black church is still trying to heal from over 400 years of chattel slavery, we are constantly re-traumatized by systematic racism that manifests in police brutality, denied opportunities, and unfair pay despite the fact that we have the same educational background and skills as our white counterparts.

You will never know the meaning of utter darkness until you have lain in such a dungeon, knowing that sunlight is streaming overhead and still only darkness below. You might have thought I was in the grip of a fantasy brought on by worry. I did worry. But there was more to the blackness than a phenomenon conjured up by a worried mind. Whatever the cause, the fact remained that I could not see the light.[127]

The state of the Black Church's mental health is in a chronic state of re-traumatization daily due to the unmet expectations of Congress, the government, U.S. presidents, white supremacist churches, and even the lack of involvement from other Black churches that don't believe in therapy for Kingdom believers. The suicide of unmet expectations has taken its toll on us. While we have experienced some liberties since the civil rights movement, Dr. King's words still ring true: "the Negro still is not free."[128] While we are able to drink from water fountains with no signs, ride in the front of the bus, and have the right to vote, racism is still felt in our communities

Keeping Hope Alive While Dying Inside

In 2018, a waitress at IHOP in Maine asked a group of Black teens for their meal.[129] In 2022, a Black woman wanted to celebrate her birthday at Chili's restaurant; however, she wasn't served until she paid upfront.[130] About one in five (21%) Black postsecondary students reports feeling discriminated against at their institutions.[131] According to the Bureau of Labor Statistics (BLS) data, the median weekly earnings for Black workers ages 16 and older are $878, compared to $1,059 for all U.S. workers in the same age group. The median weekly earnings are $823 for Hispanic workers, $1,085 for white workers, and $1,401 for Asian workers.[132]

This explains why the hope of people of color has lain in the Black Church for decades. The Black Church is an entity that many trust to plead the cause of the voiceless and unheard. Hanes Walton, Jr., professor of political science at the University of Michigan, states:

"In my doctoral work in Political Science at the University of Michigan, I have analyzed sermons delivered in historically and majority-white U.S. Christian congregations. I find that sermons infrequently mention racism: roughly 8% of sermons in my sample mention the words 'racism,' 'racist,' or 'racial.' I also find only small distinctions across denominations. When clergy talk about racism, it is more frequently the case that racism and its perceived solutions are understood in individualistic rather than systemic terms. However, a few sermons do discuss racism as a more systemic issue and call for the pursuit of racial equality."[133]

The Black church must not remain silent on the ontological issue of racism, which has devastating effects on the mental health of Black individuals. Our Black

The Black church must not remain silent on the ontological issue of racism, which has devastating effects on the mental health of Black individuals.

clergy must first challenge their biases regarding clinical counseling and understand the subconscious and conscious effects that racism has on their mental well-being. Then, and only then, will we be able to assist our parishioners in the Black church who are quietly contemplating suicide, have attempted suicide in the past, or have a suicide note in the back of their Bible.

CHAPTER FIVE

"You're Not Helping"

"Church taught me how to hate myself."
—Bishop Anthony Giyard

Before we delve into this chapter, I want to take the time to explain what is meant when the term "the Black Church" is used. According to United States Senator for Georgia and Pastor of the historically significant Ebenezer Baptist Church, Dr. Raphael G. Warnock defines the Black Church as "the varied ecclesial groupings of Christians of African descent, inside and outside Black and white denominations, imbued with the memory of a suffering Jesus and informed by the legacy of slavery and segregation in America."[134]

The Black Church was birthed out of the African understanding that Yahweh is a God of justice who does not discriminate based on race, color, or geography. Black slaves understood that "God is not one to show partiality" (Acts 10:34, NASB). However, the Bible was used by white slave owners to brainwash people of color into complying with the slave master, convincing them that chattel slavery was the will of God on earth and that heaven would be their reward. One cannot discuss chattel slavery without acknowledging the role that religion played in it.

Warnock contends:

Black Christians saw clearly the contradiction
between their status and worth in the divine

economy and their social status in a so-called Christian nation. No one embodied this belief more clearly and courageously than Harriet Tubman, abolitionist, liberator, and member of the AME Zion Church, who escaped slavery and risked her own life during some nineteen return trips to the South in order to free hundreds of slaves. Reflecting on the theological meaning of her witness, pastoral theologians Edward and Ann Wimberly have observed that 'the desire for social deliverance burned deep in her breast along with the desire for personal salvation.' Personal and social salvation mutually influenced each other in the slave tradition.[135]

The fight for freedom and racial equality is still ongoing in the 21st century, with the Black Church at the forefront. From the marches led by Reverend Al Sharpton, who founded the National Action Network, to the town hall meetings of various Black churches across the globe, the Black Church refuses to lose faith in the Word of God that states, "Learn to do good; seek justice, rebuke the oppressor, obtain justice for the orphan, plead the cause of the widow" (Isaiah 1:17, NASB). The Black Church knows that "this gospel of the Kingdom shall be preached in the whole world for a testimony to all the nations" (Matthew 24:14, NASB).

The Black Church understands what the King of Kings requires of us: that we do justice, love kindness, and walk humbly with our God (Micah 6:8). While many believe that racism is a thing of the past, people of color are not ignorant of the subliminal verbalizations of white supremacy, unjust police brutality, unfair pay, discrimination based on race, and the refusal of many whites to acknowledge that the wealth of America is attributed to the labor of people of color. **While we are still protesting as the Black Church against the discrimination that remains alive in the world, the Black Church has not screamed loudly** enough to fight for the consequences of over 400 years of slavery: trauma and suicidality.

TRAUMA & PSYCHIATRY

It is no secret that people of color have a bias against therapy and often look to the Black Church as their psychiatrists. History has proven that the fields of psychology and psychiatry have not always been kind to people of color. Dr. Jennifer Mullan has expressed her concerns regarding this sad reality:

> While we are still protesting as the Black Church against the discrimination that remains alive in the world, the Black Church has not screamed loudly enough to fight for the consequences of over 400 years of slavery: trauma and suicidality.

Racial trauma is so often pathologized, rather than acknowledged or integrated into an empowered healing paradigm. Advancing beyond individual-level approaches to coping with racial trauma, psychologically and sociologically, for BIPOC folks is essential. Research has shown that POC have been inappropriately pathologized by being incorrectly diagnosed with mental illness based on a psychologist's or psychiatrist's lack of understanding of the context in which a person of color has lived.[136]

> It is vital that people of color see more licensed therapists, psychologists, and psychiatrists who understand the state of mental health in the Black Church and the Black community.

It is vital that people of color see more licensed therapists, psy-

chologists, and psychiatrists who understand the state of mental health in the Black Church and the Black community. While trauma is discussed on a myriad of platforms today, racial trauma is often ignored when people of color seek therapy. Therapists of color who provide therapy to Blacks must understand the systemic inequality prevalent within the nucleus of psychological research.[137]

Dr. Mullan further states:

> Frankly, when I read the Willie Lynch Letter and the Making of a Slave and other historical forms of gaslighting, emotional oppression, and mind control, I am reminded of the heavy hand that psychology and psychiatry played in maintaining and creating vulnerable populations that were then labeled as 'at-risk' populations. I wonder which came first: psychology, or slave owners who created psychological frameworks. Perhaps they are one and the same. As we know, the ongoing harm still continues, as this book is birthed in the wake of the grief and rage related to the deep harm our fields have and continue to cause, in the name of 'science, research, and safety.'[138]

As a clergy member in the Black Church and a licensed counselor with a Doctor of Christian Counseling and Psychology, I am disappointed with the proven fact that most of what is written in the Diagnostic and Statistical Manual of Mental Disorders (DSM-5) does not address the historical and racial trauma of people of color. Mullan mentions in her book, Decolonizing Therapy:

> In 2021, the APA Council of Representatives recently apologized to BIPOC for their role in 'promoting, perpetuating, and failing to chal-

lenge racism, racial discrimination, and human hierarchy' in the Resolution (Auguste et al., 2021). Although this is a step toward acknowledging the perpetuation and upholding of white supremacy over hundreds of years, this apology arrives quite late. Over two hundred Black psychologists in the late '60s formed the oldest independent ethnic group: the Association of Black Psychologists (ABPsi). The protest — to engage in less harmful practices; to commit to equality and diversity as a priority, better yet as a public health issue; to commit to taking a stand against bigotry and institutional oppression; to acknowledge the historical and current-day harm that psychology has engaged in — has not been heeded.[139]

The truth of the matter is that Blacks who go to therapy are often overmedicated, due to the pharmaceutical industry having a strong influence in the revision process and raising the proclivity to medicalize patterns of moods and behaviors that are not deemed to be necessarily extreme.[140] Mullan points out, "According to the APA, antidepressant medications rank third in pharmaceutical sales worldwide, with $13.4 billion in sales last year. Additionally, antipsychotic medications generated $6.5 billion in revenue (Sharfstein, 2005)."[141]

If white therapists are not abreast of the ways in which the Black community and the Black Church mask their pain, how will they know how to properly diagnose it? **The Black Church is in desperate need of therapy because it is misunderstood by white therapists and psychologists, overrepresented by the pharmaceutical companies that overmedicate, and sadly minimized by the Black Church itself, which often downplays the need for therapy.**

Mental Health Condemned from the Pulpit

9 On one occasion, Hannah got up after they ate and drank at Shiloh. The priest Eli was sitting on a chair by the doorpost of the Lord's temple. 10 Deeply hurt, Hannah prayed to the Lord and wept with many tears. 11 Making a vow, she pleaded, "Lord of Armies, if you will take notice of your servant's affliction, remember and not forget me, and give your servant a son, I will give him to the Lord all the days of his life, and his hair will never be cut." 12 While she continued praying in the Lord's presence, Eli watched her mouth. 13 Hannah was praying silently, and though her lips were moving, her voice could not be heard. Eli thought she was drunk 14 and said to her, "How long are you going to be drunk? Get rid of your wine!" 15 "No, my lord," Hannah replied. "I am a woman with a broken heart. I haven't had any wine or beer; I've been pouring out my heart before the Lord. 16 Don't think of me as a wicked woman; I've been praying from the depth of my anguish and resentment." (1 Samuel 1:9–15, CSB)

One cannot help but notice the psychological presentation of Hannah in prayer and her response to the priest, Eli, who falsely accused her of being drunk. Hannah was unable to have children when we were first introduced to her, which deeply hurt her. However, her pain did not stop her from going to the Temple. Her troubles were expressed through behavioral symptoms of crying and lips moving with no words coming out of her mouth, which were a manifestation of a bigger issue at home:

4 Whenever Elkanah offered a sacrifice, he always gave portions of the meat to his wife Peninnah

and to each of her sons and daughters. 5 But he gave a double portion to Hannah, for he loved her even though the Lord had kept her from conceiving. 6 Her rival would taunt her severely just to provoke her, because the Lord had kept Hannah from conceiving. 7 Year after year, when she went up to the Lord's house, her rival taunted her in this way. Hannah would weep and would not eat. 8 "Hannah, why are you crying?" her husband, Elkanah, would ask. "Why won't you eat? Why are you troubled? Am I not better to you than ten sons?"
(1 Samuel 1:4-8, CSB)

It is clear that despite having a good husband, Hannah was depressed. She fits the criteria due to her change in appetite and excessive crying. Elkanah was trying to help but couldn't seem to comprehend Hannah's depression. The other woman in the house, Peninnah, had taunted Hannah for quite a while because she was able to give Elkanah what Hannah could not. One can see why Hannah prayed to such an extent in the Temple. Hannah, like the Black Church, has a worship experience that is highly misunderstood by those who relegate it to culture.

Warnock states, "Through the nineteenth-century black church's primary function as refuge—providing a spiritual respite and safe harbor from the violence and terror of white supremacy—and through its antislavery efforts, among black Baptists, for example, at the level of the local congregation, association, and denomination."[142] Clearly, the Black Church was a therapeutic fellowship for people of color, giving them a break for a few hours on Sunday morning from the ongoing reality of oppression.

The Black Church provided "a subjugated people an anti-racist institutional alternative, a church where they knew themselves to be the people of God."[145] The Black Church was the only therapeutic entity that people of color could afford. Williams contends:

> *Black folk are people of faith. About 85 percent of us identify ourselves as either fairly religious or very religious… Of the religious among us, most call themselves Christian; of those, a great many are churchgoers, and many of those who aren't churchgoers now have been before (and may be again—'cause I believe!). That's why the church can play a big role in our thinking and in our lives, and not only on Sundays—just think about that portable church known as 'prayer!'*[144]

Tragically, while the Black Church is still fighting for the rights of Blacks, the mental health struggles and suicides of its parishioners are going undetected. The Great Commission of King Jesus Christ was to take the gospel of the Kingdom to ALL nations (Matthew 28:19). It is my strong belief that one of the best ways to bring lost souls of people of color in the Black Church—those involved in gang violence, prostitution, poverty, and low-income housing—is to bring the gospel of the Kingdom to the pain of their mental health.

BLACK PEOPLE ARE TIRED OF TALKING

My grandmother used to say, "Charity begins at home." The sad reality for people of color is that we don't feel at home in America. In fact, Dr. Degruy states:

> The colonial history, the legacy of enslavement, racial subordination and segregation, racial terrorism, and racial inequality in the U.S. remain serious challenges, as there has been no real commitment to reparations and to truth and reconciliation for people of African descent.… Contemporary police killings and the trauma they create are reminiscent of the

racial terror lynchings in the past. Impunity for state violence has resulted in the current human rights crisis and must be addressed as a matter of urgency.[145]

The truth is that while many textbooks in our educational system do not teach about the pain and agony of people of color, it doesn't stop Blacks from discussing it on blogs, podcasts, social media, during marches, and from the Black pulpit. While White America endeavors to hide our history, they cannot erase the pain that is embodied in our traumatized bodies. The truth of the matter is that hurt people hurt people. Like Peninnah taunted Hannah at home, people of color have turned on each other in devastating ways.

Domestic violence is a classic trauma among people of color. Dr. Poussaint postulates:

> If you visit a local prison, you'll find that a disproportionately high percentage of those inside—men and women—have been victims of child abuse, including sexual abuse. Studies find a strong correlation between being abused and committing abuse. There is a real cycle of violence here. With the high rates of violence, suicide, and homicide among Black youth, those of you with children in your care should be extremely cautious about any kind of punishment—especially beatings—that produces anger and encourages violence in children. Homes should be a sanctuary for love and peace, not a hotbed of anger and violence.[146]

Even among our own people, we don't feel safe. We are afraid of White America and some of our own in Black America. Even in our own homes, we aren't always safe. Dr. Moody writes:

Blacks are not safe anywhere. No other race of people has had to worry about someone walking into their apartment and shooting them as they relax in the comfort of their own home; this is what a police officer did in September 2018 to Botham Jean in Dallas, Texas, making national and international news. Black people used to be afraid on the streets, and they used to be afraid only at night. Now the fear isn't relegated to any particular time of day. Because of the rash of police shootings, in which Black people are killed at their hands, any time a police officer turns on his lights, we are gripped with fear—day or night. No other race has to deal with such a psychological burden.[147]

When people don't feel safe, they do not trust. When one does not trust, they do not talk. However, what isn't discussed in the Black Church and Black community will be acted out in our behavior. People of color have felt unheard for decades. Despite the marches, conferences, affirmative action, the "Poor People's Campaign," and even book publishing, people of color feel overlooked, neglected, and most of all, unheard. I will now use the remaining part of this chapter to discuss the various manifestations of trauma in the Black community and Black Church that are desperate cries for help.

What Is the Black Male Ego Really Hiding?

Not only is America not a safe place for many of our Black males, but home isn't either. Black males have grown up in environments filled with violence, molestation, poverty, and low-income housing. Additionally, some of our Black males have been emasculated in their childhood to the extent that it affects how they think, feel, and behave today, all in the name of "I'm good." Three major areas where Black males act out what isn't talked about are violence, sex, and drug addiction.

Dr. Poussaint points out that "Black youths are six times more likely to die from homicide than white youths and seven times more likely to commit a homicide. During the last thirty years, close to 50 percent of the homicides in the United States have been committed by Black people, mostly Black men, and 94 percent of the victims of Black killers were Black."[148] Why is this something for the Black church to take seriously? Many of our young Black males are out in the streets while their parents and grandparents are in church on Sunday morning.

Furthermore, another reason why violence in the Black community should be taken seriously is due to the link between Black homicide and suicide. According to lead author Daniel Semenza, director of interpersonal violence research at the New Jersey Gun Violence Research Center, "Our study found that exposure to gun violence, whether experienced directly or indirectly, is associated with increased suicidal thoughts and behaviors among Black adults."[149] The sad truth is that instead of recognizing the hopelessness and silence of our Black youth, we penalize the symptoms of their silence while not mandating that they go to therapy and deal with the root of their diagnosis.

Additionally, what the Black church must realize is that homicide and suicide in the Black community are more than just crimes stemming from the inner trauma of people of color; they also reflect the culture. Dr. Poussaint further argues:

The homicide problem is so out of control that some pundits have suggested that these killings are part of the 'culture' of the Black poor. Gangsta rappers glorify violence to young Black teens. Many—in a twisted way—may feel they gain status among their friends by shooting someone, even if they go to jail for years or even for life. Some teens have been killing themselves with firearms instead of killing others. As a result, the suicide rate has risen among young Black males in the past three decades to approach the rate for all young males combined.[150]

> **Black males are using sex as a way to mask their pain. The sexuality of Black males cannot be understood outside the confines of racism.**

Secondly, **Black males are using sex as a way to mask their pain. The sexuality of Black males cannot be understood outside the confines of racism.** The strong correlation between racism and sexuality accentuates the Black male's desire to synchronize lust and power. According to Lipscomb:

For Black men, race and racism are inextricably linked to sexuality (Bowleg et al., 2017). Viewed within a historical context, sexuality is a fundamental element in the ongoing oppression and marginalization of Black men. Bowleg et al. (2017) outlined several historic periods, including: slavery (the racist stereotypes of Black men as virile with a rabid lust for White women); post-slavery (the lynching of Black men for raping White women, despite a lack of evidence to support these accusations).[151]

A. L. Reynolds postulates, "Sex is the one thing most Black men believe they can control. From slavery through Reconstruction, the Black male was conditioned to believe that the only domain that belonged to him alone was sex."[152] Well into the twenty-first century, many of our Black males believe that having more women will enhance their self-esteem. Nothing could be further from the truth. Furthermore, sexuality is a vital matter to be addressed in the Black church, especially due to the rise in HIV and AIDS.

It has been the reality of the Black church that Black males in our churches are losing their lives to HIV and AIDS. Award-winning journalist for the *Washington Post*, Brandon Ambrosino, states:

> Since the early 2000s, the topic of Black men who have sex with men but identify as straight has been heavily discussed in major American media outlets. Public interest in the topic only intensified when journalists connected the DL[153] phenomenon to HIV infection rates in the Black communities, which are disproportionately higher than among whites. In a 2006 book, Pastor Michael Stevens called the down low an 'invisible disease' plaguing Black churches and outlined a plan of healing for those Black men who wanted out.[154]

To understand the plight of Black males is to understand the ways in which they act out their depression and anxiety, which is often through sex. Bishop T. D. Jakes once remarked in a sermon entitled He-Motions, "Sex is not a sign a man is happy." While the topic of sexuality is a taboo subject in many traditional Black churches, the percentage of men on the "down low" is rising, infecting women with multiple sexually transmitted infections (STIs).

To understand the plight of Black males is to understand the ways in which they act out their depression and anxiety, which is often through sex.

While HIV and AIDS can affect any race, culture, or ethnicity, the statistics are particularly high among people of color. According to the CDC, men who have sex with men accounted for 70% of the 32,100 estimated new infections in 2021, even though they made up only 2% of the population, with the highest burden among Black and Latino gay and bisexual men.[155] Additionally, "The rate of new HIV infections among Black women is 10 times that of white women and four times that of Latina women."[156] The Black church must address this sad reality because our pews are filled with members of the LGBTQ community.

According to journalist Keith Boykin, "Many of our Black churches would stop running if the gay, lesbian, and bisexual members dropped out."[157] While the church is not to condone sin on any level, addressing the mental health of the sinner is a crucial tool that can lead to repentance. We must remember, as in the case of the woman caught in the act of adultery, that Christ addressed her sin but also told her, "Neither do I condemn you; go, and from now on sin no more" (John 8:11, ESV). It is estimated that:

> Among Black transgender and nonbinary young people, those who were assigned female at birth reported higher rates of both seriously considering suicide in the past year (60%) and attempting suicide in the past year (26%) com-

pared to Black transgender and nonbinary young people. There were no significant differences between Black young people who were transgender and Black young people who were nonbinary in any assessed mental health indicators.[158]

While we must address sin, we must also "speak the truth in love" (Ephesians 4:15) simultaneously. Being in sin should not disqualify any sinner from experiencing the love of God from the people of God. In fact, God reminds us that we draw the unbeliever through lovingkindness (Jeremiah 31:3). Christ made it clear that "God did not send His Son into the world to condemn the world, but to save the world through Him" (John 3:17, NIV). The apostle addresses the issue by stating:

> *9 Or do you not know that wrongdoers will not inherit the kingdom of God? Do not be deceived: Neither the sexually immoral nor idolaters nor adulterers nor men who have sex with men 10 nor thieves nor the greedy nor drunkards nor slanderers nor swindlers will inherit the kingdom of God. 11 And that is what some of you were. But you were washed, you were sanctified, you were justified in the name of the Lord Jesus Christ and by the Spirit of our God. (1 Corinthians 6:9-11, NIV)*

Lastly, drug addiction is another fatal coping mechanism utilized by Black males. While drug addiction affects all ages, races, and demographics, our Black males often numb their pain with drugs and alcohol. "In early 2018, 42% of U.S. adults said drug addiction was a major problem in their community, but that percentage declined to 35% in October 2021. Around four-in-ten Black adults (42%) said in the 2021 survey that drug addiction was a major problem in their community, compared with smaller shares of White (34%) and Asian adults (20%)."[159]

> **Maybe we are so focused on their sin that we have forgotten that sinners have pain too. If we can help our Black males get out of the drug-dealing business, they can focus on the Father's business.**

The Black church must get involved with the Black males we pass by on the way to church every Sunday. Maybe we are afraid to approach them due to how they are dressed and the "game face" displayed on their countenance. Perhaps we are consumed with our own pain and church obligations. **Maybe we are so focused on their sin that we have forgotten that sinners have pain too. If we can help our Black males get out of the drug-dealing business, they can focus on the Father's business.**

"The Angry Black Woman" Could Be Suicidal

It was reported that "suicide rates among Black women increased from 1999 to 2020, especially among teens and adults, according to an analysis of national data. Among Black women ages 15 to 84, suicide rates rose from 2.1 per 100,000 in 1999 to 3.4 per 100,000 in 2020, according to Victoria Joseph, MPH, of the Columbia University Mailman School of Public Health in New York, and colleagues."[160] These statistics are alarming and concerning. We must remember that Black women are significant supporters of the Black church.

Society views the Black woman as "angry," "ghetto," and "high-maintenance." Truth be told, it's difficult to understand anyone that we label. I once heard leadership expert John C. Maxwell say that 90% of inmates were told growing up that they would end up in jail. Are our Black women angry without a cause? Anger is a secondary emotion. Thus, we must address the underlying issues that plague Black women today. Terrie M. Williams assists us in understanding the hurt and mental health challenges underneath Black women's pain:

> Being Black and being a woman makes us more vulnerable to all negative aspects of our society—poverty, poor health, single parenting, HIV, and homelessness—which makes us even more vulnerable to things like abuse, workplace harassment, incarceration, and drugs… Women are generally more victimized, and victimized more often, than men, so there's a greater likelihood that we'll be victims in general. We're especially more likely to be victims of domestic abuse and sexual abuse and to be targeted as easy marks for crime.[161]

One can understand why Black women fill the Black church to capacity. It is the one place where they believe their emotions are safe. However, safe doesn't always mean secure. While the Black church has provided a safe space for Black women to express themselves, we have failed to supply the necessary resources and referrals to assist them with mental health and suicidality. Hannah went to church to express her emotions in prayer. However, the priest Eli did not understand her, nor did he know how to address her.

Many in the Black church are made to believe that their depression and anxiety can be dealt with through prayer alone. Other times, the mental health of those in the Black church is attributed to sin. Professor and author Dr. Tasia Scrutton argues, "Sin accounts of depression can also be damaging in less direct ways. For example, they can deflect attention from the social and psychological causes of mental illness. They can discourage people from seeking medical and psychological help that may be therapeutic and even life-saving."[162]

Hannah had to deal with another woman in the house who taunted her and a well-meaning husband who didn't understand her. The last place she needs to be misunderstood is in the house of the Living God. Eli accuses her of being "drunk" rather than being emotionally distressed. Eli is not alone in his false allegations. Western culture, the media, and even the Black church do not understand the pain behind the "angry Black woman." While women of color have a multiplicity of coping skills to mask their anger, we will address three main coping skills.

Weight problems are common in women of color as a coping mechanism for stress and mental health issues. One common reason why struggles with weight gain aren't given much attention is due to society's stereotypes of the "thick Black chick" and the "skinny white girl." Winters points out, "Even though 80 percent of Black women are classified as overweight according to body mass index standards, based on a number of studies, Black women are satisfied with their bodies and are motivated to lose weight based on health-related concerns, not Western standards of beauty. As a matter of fact, larger body frames are more often viewed positively than negatively."[163]

While some Black women are confident in their weight, a significant number are insecure about their body image. In fact, this is a common issue for Black women in the Black church. In Hollywood, when movie producers want an actress to emulate Black women in the Black church, they are sure to cast an actress who is not only Black but overweight. This phenomenon was exemplified in the 2000 comedy film *Big Momma's House*. Martin Lawrence plays the role of an FBI agent disguising himself as an overweight, God-fearing Black grandmother. While the Black community and Black church look up to and respect "Big Momma," we often neglect the fact that "Big Momma's" weight could be covering underlying depression from being the family's matriarch, bailing her son out of jail, raising her daughter's kids while their mom battles drug addiction, and so much more.

Licensed clinical psychotherapist Nadine A. Thompson struggles with being the good church girl who battles with weight. Williams narrates her story:

> Nadine recalls witnessing a phenomenon in her early adult years where her girlfriends who wanted to keep their weight down were doing other drugs and finding other ways to manage their weight and anxiety. For Nadine, she had to maintain the facade of being a good girl for her very conservative parents. It was okay to have a chocolate bar but not okay to light up a cigarette; it was okay to cook a huge dinner and dessert for the family but not to pour a drink or get stoned.[164]

In an endeavor to keep her conservative parents happy while avoiding drugs, Nadine resorted to food. Interestingly enough, Nadine saw this same issue with her Black female clients:

> Later in her clinical practice with young women, she saw the same pattern for young Black women, especially those involved in their church. If they were struggling with anxiety, emotional or sexual abuse, depression, or emotional distress, food became an acceptable addiction. No one judged your character based on your weight or the extra serving of fried chicken you ate. The problem was that the fat girls were the last to get a date or get married, so the irony was that you were being judged 'as good enough or not' as opposed to whether you were a 'bad or good girl.'[165]

Food is definitely "comfort food" in the Black church and among our Black women. Additionally, eating disorders such as bulimia and anorexia are often associated with white women. However, research shows that these disorders also affect women of color. According to the Boston Medical Center, "Black women are less likely than white women to seek eating disorder treatment, and even when engaged, are more likely to drop out. It is the responsibility of clinicians to reform approaches to treatment that address the psychopathology of the motivation behind binge eating in Black women for optimal treatment retention."[166] One of the contributing factors to Black women overeating as a coping mechanism leads us to our second common coping skill among women of color in the Black church: overworking.

Black women on Sunday mornings don't look depressed. One can find them dressed in their Sunday best, giving God "the highest praise." Winters states:

> 'Just pray on it' is often the advice that Black women give each other and others to deal with life's burdens. Strong belief in an omnipotent, omniscient, omnipresent God who would never leave us or forsake us is how many of us endure. The Black church is a place of refuge where you know your Blackness is unconditionally accepted; you are uplifted and supported, and you leave Sunday service with the strength to survive another week. 'Faith without works is dead' (James 2:26). It is the combination of our faith and persistent work for justice that has brought us this far. Black women are able to thrive in spite of centuries of denigration.[167]

While it is true that Black women are succeeding in the face of "centuries of denigration," the real question is how are Black women coping with the stress of being a "Strong Black woman"? Many of our Black women are stressed out from trying to be successful while being single mothers. Furthermore, despite climbing the corporate ladder, Black women are still not bringing in more income. Winters points out, "Black women, on average, earn sixty-two cents for every dollar that a white man earns. White women make eighty-two cents for every dollar a white man earns. The higher level of education does not change the wage gaps. Among doctorate degree holders, for instance, Black women earn 60 percent of what white men do, and white women earn 7 percent more than Black women."[168]

Lastly, to reward themselves for being overworked, some Black women's third coping skill is overspending. Williams states:

> It won't surprise you to hear that a lot of us have overspending as our drug of choice. We might pat ourselves on the back for how clean we live— don't smoke, drink, do drugs, cuss, or cheat; hit the gym three times a week; go to church on Sunday—but we use shopping to 'take the edge off' the same way other sisters gotta have that drink or light up that joint the second they walk in the door. Call us shopaholics, spendthrifts, compulsive shoppers… Whatever we're called, just like a compulsive eater, we can take something perfectly natural and even necessary (a girl's gotta wear clothes, right?) and use it to numb ourselves against feelings and pain we don't know how to handle.[169]

Thus, **we must understand that Black women in the Black church and Black community are struggling with depression, emotional distress, and even suicidal ide-**

We must understand that Black women in the Black church and Black community are struggling with depression, emotional distress, and even suicidal ideations that are commonly seen as "the angry Black woman" syndrome.

ations that are commonly seen as "the angry Black woman" syndrome. Like the priest Eli, who misjudged Hannah's pain for being "drunk," clergy within the Black church are misjudging the pain of Black women. Educator and author Ruth King explains the difference between anger and rage:

> Rage and anger are often regarded as the same emotion, but they are distinct experiences. Anger is primarily associated with a current injustice, dislike, or disappointment—like a driver cutting in front of you without signaling… Rage is an accumulation of anger, an experience that is primarily physical and rooted in unresolved or unknown trauma that shamed us in childhood. Rage is a visceral and instinctive response when we feel we have little or no control over what is threatening or harassing us.[170]

Like the toll that Penninah's taunting took on Hannah, Black women in the Black church and the Black community experience the taunting of white supremacy, racism, and abuse daily that leaves them in a state of trauma (more on trauma in the next chapter). Winters argues:

> The 'angry Black woman' is probably the most fatiguing stereotype to manage. I contend that as Black women we have a lot to be angry about. Brittany J. Harris, vice president of learning and innovation at the Winters Group, put it this way in a post in our Inclusion Solution newsletter: 'I find it fascinating how I've essentially learned (internalized) that suppressing my feelings, truth, and anger (despite how much studies show this can be a detriment to my health) is worth not being characterized as or associated with being an 'Angry Black Woman.'[171]

Our Black women are in need of therapy and understanding. It is Malcolm X who once stated, in his 1962 speech, "The most disrespected person in America is the Black woman. The most unprotected person in America is the Black woman.[172] The most neglected person in America is the Black woman." The mental health of women of color is serious. As licensed trauma therapist Kobe Campbell describes one of her clients (a Black woman) dealing with depression, she states, "During our first session, Esi told me that she was anxious all the time, sharing that the only time she wasn't anxious was when she was depressed."[173] Understanding our Black women requires first understanding their childhood trauma.

"SAVE THE CHILDREN"

Often within the Black church, the depression and emotional distress in children are seldom discussed. This tragedy stems from the Black folktale that "children are seen and not heard." Growing up in Black families, many of us were used to hearing phrases like, "Stop crying before I give you something to cry about," "Stay in a child's place," and "You're lazy." In most Black churches, a teenager's rebellious behavior, which could be a manifestation of "acting out" depression, is addressed from the pulpit before their unhealthy self-esteem and the mental health issues that drive it are acknowledged.

Williams contends:

> The biggest stumbling block to treating youth depression is that we ignore the signs of pain until the symptoms become public problems— instead we use catchall terms like "at risk" that mask how many teens are suffering the effects of depression. Depression in young people is ten times more common than it was two generations ago. Since 1980, the rate of suicide

for Black boys ages fifteen to nineteen has sky-rocketed. A study reported in the New York Times showed that in 342 detention centers around the country, there were 15,000 emotionally disturbed teens with no mental health care resources to address their psychological issues. What happens to them? They're warehoused in juvenile centers and prisons.[174]

In the Black church, we have youth departments, children's church, and even one Sunday out of the month dedicated to "Youth Sunday." However, how many of our youth departments and Youth Sunday services address the insecurities, trauma, and suicidality of our Black children who are wrestling with confusing feelings that they struggle to voice but have no problem acting out? Dr. Tamar Mendelson argues that "there is a mental, emotional, and behavioral health crisis for children in our country... we need to address the structural and systemic issues that threaten our young people's well-being; at the same time, there is a lot we can be doing to decrease risk factors for families."[175]

In Marvin Gaye's 1971 song "Save the children," he sings:

When I look at the world
It fills me with sorrow
Little children today
Are really gonna suffer tomorrow
(Oh!) What a shame
Such a bad way to live
Oh, who is to blame?
We can't stop living
(Ohhh!) Live, (Live)
(Live for life) Live for life
(But let live everybody)
Live life for the children

In order for the Black church to help our children, we must first address the wounds of the child within. We must seek to understand ourselves—not just as Saints, but as people of color who don't feel accepted in a world full of racism while feeling misunderstood on Sunday mornings. Christ said to His disciples, "Let the children come to me; do not hinder them, for to such belongs the kingdom of God" (Mark 10:14, ESV). The Black church, like the disciples, must understand that Christ wanted to "touch" the children. Many of our Black children have been touched by racism, molestation, child abuse, and much more. How can they experience Christ's touch when Black churches ignore their mental health?

> In order for the Black church to help our children, we must first address the wounds of the child within.

When people don't feel understood, they feel rejected. When they feel rejected, they feel alone. When they feel alone, they feel depressed. When they feel depressed, they may cope in the wrong way (even in church). If they cope in the wrong way, one of those coping skills may be suicide. This leads us to the next type of suicide in the Black church: the suicide of the rejected and misunderstood. Let's go to the next chapter and discuss this.

CHAPTER SIX

King Jesus Doesn't Just Heal the Body

"The Spirit of the Lord Yahweh is upon me...
He sent me to bind up the brokenhearted."
—Isaiah 61:1 (LSB)

Sometimes I wonder if the Black church has forgotten why we exist. Please understand that although I am addressing "the Black church," I want us to be mindful that the church is not based on color. Due to segregation and discrimination stemming from racism, the Black church was birthed. This does not negate the fact that the Black church is a part of the Body of Christ. However, we must not forget that the objective of the church is to "make disciples of all nations" (Matthew 28:19, ESV). Additionally, we must remember that making disciples in the Black community and the Black church also means addressing our mental health as well.

The Scriptures are clear that Christ our King came to heal the brokenhearted (Isaiah 61:1). However, one must realize that in Scripture, the heart and mind are used interchangeably. Dr. Jacqueline McCullough states, "The heart is also viewed as the seat of emotions... The heart is the housing place of our thoughts, feelings, desires, hopes, dreams, pain, and disappointment, to name a few. The Greek word for 'heart' is kardia (kar-dee'-ah), which refers to 'the thoughts or feelings of the mind.' It is impossible to separate one's feelings or thoughts from one's mind."[176]

In the Black church, we are renowned for addressing the heart while forgetting that in the Hebraic Scriptures, the mind is taken into consideration when the heart is mentioned. Furthermore, when the mind is addressed in the Black church, quick solutions are offered in the sermonic theatrics of "shake off that depression" or "come out of that low self-esteem." Without a clinical understanding of depression, anxiety, and low self-worth—which are the ingredients for suicidality—we will do our parishioners more harm than good. One cannot get rid of type two diabetes by metaphorically "shaking it off" in church on Sunday morning. They must exercise and make the proper lifestyle changes to their nutrition. By the same token, our parishioners in the Black church should be referred to licensed counselors and psychologists who believe in faith-based therapeutic interventions

In the Black church, we are renowned for addressing the heart while forgetting that in the Hebraic Scriptures, the mind is taken into consideration when the heart is mentioned.

The Mind & Body of Traumatized Blacks

In order for us to better assist our congregants in the Black church, we must understand trauma from a clinical lens. While the term trauma is used daily to describe how we feel, it's vital to understand that everything is not trauma. Licensed trauma therapist Antonieta Contrera contends:

> Trauma always refers to the effects of the activation of the innate survival circuits that are designed to protect the individual from the possibility of dying after a severe reaction to a threatening occurrence. Trauma, in the strictest

sense of the construct, is connected to severity—severity in the precipitating event, in the reaction, and the aftermath. This is important. For trauma to be a thing in anyone's life, the person has to have been exposed to a severe event or circumstance that pushed their brain to use exaggerated measures to guarantee survival, causing severe consequences to their system.[177]

Racial trauma is more than an event for Blacks; it's a daily recurrence and reminder that we are not wanted by white America.

Interestingly enough, what qualifies someone to have gone through trauma is the severity of the precipitating event or a severe event that leaves the individual on guard and always in survival mode. The problem with the above description, while accurate, does not take into account the specialized trauma of people of color. That trauma is coined as racial trauma. Racial trauma refers to the mental and emotional injury caused by encounters with racial bias and ethnic discrimination, racism, and hate crimes.[178] **Racial trauma is more than an event for Blacks; it's a daily recurrence and reminder that we are not wanted by white America.** Menakem postulates:

In America, nearly all of us, regardless of our background or skin color, carry trauma in our bodies around the myth of race. We typically think of trauma as the result of a specific and deeply painful event, such as a serious accident, an attack, or the news of someone's death. That may be the case sometimes, but trauma can also be the body's response to a long sequence of smaller wounds. It can be a response to anything that it experiences as too much, too soon, or too fast.[179]

Racial trauma has also been referred to as colonization by Dr. Jennifer Mullan. She states, "Colonization is a psychological and spiritual trauma. Colonization and its effects are traumatic and can cause continued trauma. There have been numerous definitions of colonization. One definition is the systematic and methodical removal of land, culture, trust (in self and others), family, history, freedom, and spirit."[180] I contend that the trauma of Black people is different from the trauma of whites. I am not alone in this conviction. Dr. DeGruy's research supports my argument.

Dr. DeGruy coined the term *post-traumatic slave syndrome (PTSS)*. She defines PTSS as "a multigenerational trauma together with continued oppression and absence of opportunity to access the benefits available in society lead to… Post-Traumatic Slave Syndrome."[181] Notice that in Mullan and DeGruy's definitions, both mention the continued trauma and continued oppression of Blacks. While the goal of therapy is to assist individuals with coping skills and new techniques to deal with past or current issues that caused post-traumatic stress disorder (PTSD), **people of color live in a retraumatizing society that makes us feel defeated and dejected. Our post-traumatic stress disorder is really post-traumatic slave syndrome.**

This continued oppression ultimately takes its toll on the physiology of Blacks. Dr. Moody notes:

> When we experience stress, our body releases cortisol, also known as 'the stress hormone.' The release of cortisol sends a message to the blood: leave the core of the body and go to the extremities, because we might have to move quickly in response to this stressor. Cortisol also makes us alert by sending a message that it's not time to sleep, and it suppresses our appetite by sending a message that it's not time to eat; it's time to get ready to fight![182]

However, what happens when the body is perpetually under a state of trauma and stress? Dr. Moody continues:

> Here's the thing about stress: our bodies are wired to handle stressful situations temporarily. When we remain in stressful contexts for prolonged periods of time, the results are damaging to our bodies. The same hormones that are supposed to help us deal with stress—cortisol, norepinephrine, and epinephrine—remain in our blood, causing negative chemical reactions that shorten our life expectancy.[183]

The chronic racial trauma that Blacks live with and encounter daily stresses and destroys the body. Thus, while the Black church worships Christ "in the dance" on Sunday morning, we are constantly confronted with historical trauma when we walk outside the church doors. When a Black man experiences the adrenaline rush of anxiety as police sirens are behind him on the parkway, his life expectancy is being shortened. As Black mothers worry about their Black sons making it home safely, their life expectancy is being shortened. This continued stress and trauma lead to other health issues among people of color.

Menakem writes, "The traumas that live in Black bodies are deep and persistent. They contribute to a long list of common stress disorders in Black bodies, such as post-traumatic stress disorder (PTSD), learning disabilities, depression and anxiety, diabetes, high blood pressure, and other physical and emotional ailments."[184]

The Black church, along with Black clergy, must take our mental health very seriously because many of our physical ailments are rooted in psychological trauma. Often, the remedies for our mental health, given to us by clergy, are "Trust God," "You're not doing what God told you to do," or "Praise your way through." This is what Dr. Bryant calls spiritual bypassing. She describes spiritual bypassing as "the clinging to our identity as spiritual beings to the point of denying our human condition, hurts, or challenges—is another form of distancing and distracting."[185]

It's vital for clergy in the Black church to understand the effects of trauma on the bodies of their congregants. The effects of trauma on the body go all the way back to our childhood. Campbell asserts:

> Our childhood trauma affects us more than just psychologically and emotionally; it also affects us biologically as well, shifting the way our bodies operate, because our bodies are where experiences are stored until we identify, address, and resolve them. The biological implications of the unhealed and unaddressed pain of our childhood create the wiring of how our brains interact, which is the foundation of the patterns of our everyday lives.[186]

When the trauma of the retraumatized Black church is not taken seriously, it adds insult to the rejection we already feel from white society and even some of our own people. This leads us to the next category of suicide in the Black church: the suicide of the rejected and misunderstood.

The Suicide of the Rejected
and Misunderstood

23 "When Ahithophel realized that his advice had not been followed, he saddled his donkey and set out for his house in his hometown. He set his house in order and hanged himself. So he died and was buried in his father's tomb" (2 Samuel 17:23-25, CSB)

Ahithophel was the advisor to Absalom, King David's son. Ahithophel is upset with David for sleeping with his granddaughter, Bathsheba, and having his grandson-in-law, Uriah, killed (2 Samuel chapter 11). Absalom has his own personal grudge against his father and wants to take the throne from him. Ahithophel joins Absalom's team in an endeavor to kill David. However, the Lord ensures that Ahithophel's advice fails and is ultimately rejected by Absalom. Ahithophel finds out and kills himself because his counsel was rejected.

There are some parallels between Ahithophel and Black men. Ahithophel wants justice for his grandson-in-law and is angry with David for committing adultery with his granddaughter. For over 400 years, Black men had to watch their wives get raped by the slave master or hear their screams while they were working, knowing that they could not do anything about it. Sociologist and professor Dr. Andrew Billingsley contends, "In addition to the supreme authority of the slave master over the Black family, the slave owners and the other whites took frequent sexual advantage of the slave women… Slave husbands had to watch and not say a word while their wives were flogged."[187]

Additionally, Ahithophel has been carrying this grudge in his

> The reality speaks for itself: America is a strange land to Blacks whose labor white supremacy has made—and continues to make—profit off of.

heart against David, which explains why he wants David dead. Similarly, many people of color are angry with white supremacists—not because we want to play the victim and feel sorry for ourselves, but because we are frustrated by the fact that, regardless of our efforts to fit in while maintaining our "Blackness" and culture, we are treated as less than, without white America explicitly stating it as they did during slavery. **The reality speaks for itself: America is a strange land to Blacks whose labor white supremacy has made—and continues to make—profit off of.**

THE TRAUMA OF REJECTION

As stated earlier in this chapter, the trauma of people of color, which Dr. Degruy refers to as post-traumatic slave syndrome (PTSS), is a complex and chronic trauma. It's not trauma that happens once in a person's lifetime but a daily reality for the mind, body, and soul of people of color. Leading trauma expert, neuroscientist, and psychologist Dr. Jennifer Sweeton highlights key areas of the brain that are affected by trauma: the thalamus, the amygdala, the hippocampus, the insula, the nucleus accumbens, the anterior cingulate cortex, the ventromedial prefrontal cortex, and the dorsolateral cortex.[188] For the remainder of this chapter, we will use her expertise to exemplify the complex trauma of people of color. We will first examine the thalamus's role in the re-traumatization of Black people.

The thalamus is responsible for short-term memory and sleep. Furthermore, it has sometimes been referred to as the relay station for sensory information because one function of this brain structure is to reroute incoming sensory information.[189] The thalamus's task is to transport information to our hippocampus, which contains long-term memory, or to the amygdala.[190] Additionally, Sweeton notes, "the thalamus appears to be most involved in the re-experiencing symptoms of PTSD."[191] The thalamus facilitates flashbacks of PTSD, for example.

What does one do, however, when the flashbacks are the reality of everyday life? What do you do when you experience anxiety every day you walk out your front door because of your skin color? What do you do when you have flashbacks every time you go into the workplace, knowing that you will train others for the position you want and they don't have dark skin? The hippocampus doesn't make it better, as it is the part of the brain that deals with learning and goal-directed behavior.[192]

Sadly, too much damage done to the hippocampus will result in an inability to form new memories.[193] How does one form new memories when every day they are faced with the sad truth that their memories of yesterday mirror the state of their reality today? The hippocampus is also the stress management part of the brain. Nevertheless, people of color are struggling to manage the stress of being Black in a white-dominated world. Not too far from the hippocampus is the dorsolateral prefrontal cortex, which is responsible for reasoning, decision-making, emotion regulation, reality testing, and working memory.[194] Nevertheless, when too much damage has been done to the dorsolateral prefrontal cortex, it can cause attention difficulties and decrease motivation,[195] which may come off as laziness to others with no understanding of the effects of trauma on the brain.

Then there is the insula. This is the part of the brain that births emotion.[196] Sweeton argues, "Insula research indicates that emotion is involved in cognition. While emotion and cognition are sometimes presented as separate, opposing phenomena, the insula's role in emotional and cognitive integration suggests that emotion is part of cognition."[197] Furthermore, interoception, which is "the ability to detect, feel into, and process internal bodily states and sensations,"[198] comes before emotion. The insula plays a big role in trauma, as it affects how one trusts. Blacks live every day uncomfortable in America—feeling like the criminal justice system, insurance companies, and even white evangelicals cannot be trusted.

Dr. Phillips contends, "Trauma can even impact the heritage of culture through prejudice, disenfranchisement, and health inequities. Some historically traumatic events can be so widespread that they not only impact entire cultures but are so intense that they influence generations beyond those who experience them directly."[199] Phillips points out that "the enslavement and lynching of African Americans, the genocide in Rwanda, Japanese internment camps in America, and the Holocaust are all examples of historical trauma."[200]

> **When an individual is confined to repeated trauma in the same geographical location, distrust is also intensified.**

When an individual is confined to repeated trauma in the same geographical location, distrust is also intensified. When trust is an issue, survival becomes the goal. Many within the Black church and the Black community struggle with their goals due to the mistrust that is at the nucleus of their trauma. This leads us to the nucleus accumbens. This is the reward expectation part of the brain that impacts goal-directed behavior.[201] The nucleus accumbens prompts an individual to want to make the Dean's list in college or excel in the corporate arena. Sweeton postulates, "The nucleus accumbens produces the experience of reinforcement with the help of dopamine, which is a neurotransmitter that makes situations, people, drugs, or behaviors feel pleasant."[202]

However, after experiencing trauma, this part of the brain that is responsible for one's ability to experience satisfaction now causes them to feel depressed.[203] Now is a good time to pause in this dissertation and remind you that many African Americans have strong biases against seeking help for mental health. While over-the-counter medications like Tylenol, Aleve, or Advil are the go-to in inner-city convenience stores, they won't relieve the effects of trauma on the brain. **While praise breaks on Sunday morning may make us feel better, they don't relieve trauma on the brain.**

The Dominant Part of the Brain of the Traumatized

Now we will look at where the real damage is done in the brain: the amygdala. The amygdala is known as the fear processing center of the brain, or as it's often called, the "fear center."[204] Sweeton states, "The amygdala is considered the survival brain structure and is one of the first areas of the brain to process incoming sensory information from the body… After sensory information is processed by the thalamus, it travels to two locations: the cortex and the amygdala (Garrido et al., 2012). Notably, the amygdala receives the sensory information in about half the time it takes for the information to reach the cortex."[205]

This means that the amygdala, operating outside the awareness of consciousness, is trying to make sense of sensory information before it even reaches the rational and conscious brain areas.[206] After trauma, the amygdala appears to become hyperactive or hypoactive in response to danger. Phillips contends that the amygdala plays a vital role in learning and memory by linking emotional significance to events.[207] The hyperactive amygdala in brains exposed to trauma causes the anterior cingulate cortex (the part of the brain responsible for emotional regulation and consciousness) to be under-activated.[208]

When the anterior cingulate cortex is under-activated, those with PTSD re-experience symptoms, while the amygdala creates a startled response to non-threatening circumstances and stimuli. Sweeton writes:

> Traumatized individuals often report feeling on-guard and reactive to their environment, especially when in unfamiliar, unpredictable, or crowded situations. To those around them, these individuals may appear distracted, jumpy, and reactive. This can also be the case in the context of therapy, where the therapeutic setting may provoke anxiety in clients. These

individuals may spend substantial time scanning the room during sessions, and they often seem to have difficulty concentrating during therapy. Conversely, dissociation or emotional numbing may indicate hypoactive amygdala. Clients with a hypoactive amygdala may seem disconnected or detached from their traumas as they discuss them and may report feeling lethargic and depressed.[209]

Black trauma has a symptom called "Tired." It's common to hear people of color say, "I'm too tired to do anything," cancel outings due to being tired, or even fall asleep in church. In the Black church, there are countless songs that verbalize the tiredness of the Black struggle. Songs like, "My body is tired, and my soul needs rest. O Lord, let me lean on You," "Sit down servant and rest a little while," and "There's a leak in this ole building and my soul has got to move." However, there is a classic in the Black church that, while still sung, may not fully convey the truth of Black trauma: "I don't feel no ways tired."

Though that song was recorded by the late James Cleveland and later by Mary Mary, it doesn't mean that people of color aren't tired. In fact, during a reality show starring Mary Mary's Erica Campbell and Tina Campbell, Erica was told by her physician that she had hypertension, and she later reported she'd had a stroke.[210] Her doctor told her she needed to slow down. Additionally, both sisters believe in getting treatment for mental health.[211] The reason why many Blacks are tired and not seeking treatment is due to our home remedies for self-soothing.

The vagus nerve is one of the least discussed nerves in the body. The vagus nerve can be weakened by stress and trauma, disrupting the autonomic nervous system.[212] Menakem refers to the vagus nerve as the "soul nerve."[213] He contends, "The soul nerve is not just where we experience our emotions. It's also where we feel a sense of belonging. This is why we can think of it as both a bodily organ and a communal one. Within each human body is this deep raw aching desire."[214]

This echoes back to the suicides of the rejected and misunderstood. In the famous psychologist Abraham Maslow's hierarchy of needs, the third need is love and belonging.[215] When an individual feels like they don't belong, the most inappropriate behaviors can manifest.

IT'S OK TO BE BLACK AND TIRED

Often in the Black church and Black community, we don't allow ourselves to be tired. This also includes not giving ourselves time to deal with the tears that roll down our faces in the car, missing doctor's appointments because "I don't have time for that," ignoring migraines by "sleeping it off," and telling ourselves that Black people have to be strong. However, ignoring embodied trauma and unresolved depression doesn't make them go away.

Licensed Christian psychologist Dr. Tim Murphy postulates, "We burn out because we were just not made to carry stress and trauma forever. Our bodies are amazingly adaptive, but there is a breaking point that we cannot mentally, physically, emotionally, or spiritually endure. We can try to delay the burnout by self-medicating with alcohol, drugs, and vices. But we will not escape the impact of stress if we do not change the cause."[216] However, one must understand that the burnout people of color face goes beyond the common understanding of trauma.

People of color live with the trauma of being rejected and misunderstood. Our Black men, for instance, know this too well. **Many Black men feel rejected and misunderstood by their families, considered lazy and a "sorry excuse of a man" for not finding employment after getting out of prison. What isn't taken into consideration is how an employer turns him down after he's honest about his criminal history.** Grier and Cobbs remark:

> If the Black American is to be truly understood, his history must be made intelligible. It is a history that is interwoven with that of his country, although it is rarely reported with candor. In recent years, superficial studies of Negroes have been made. For those few who truly search, the past of the Black man is seen reflected in his daily life... The Black man of today is at one end of a psychological continuum that reaches back in time to his enslaved ancestors. Observe closely a man on a Harlem street corner, and it can be seen how little his life experience differs from that of his forebears. However much the externals differ, their inner life is remarkably the same.[217]

Many Black men feel rejected and misunderstood by their families, considered lazy and a "sorry excuse of a man" for not finding employment after getting out of prison. What isn't taken into consideration is how an employer turns him down after he's honest about his criminal history.

Years of feeling rejected and misunderstood take their toll on our emotional and physical health. Dr. Walker states:

> We neglect our emotional health the same way we neglect our physical health, except that our neglect for our emotional health is far worse. We neglect problems until the situation is dire or can no longer be avoided. If you were to break your leg, you would see a physician right away because getting around on a broken leg would be really hard to do. Because emotional problems do not shut us down, we keep going despite the potential long-term consequences.[218]

While people of color are always on the go, we carry the strain and trauma of systemic oppression, injustice, and feelings of rejection and being misunderstood within us.

While people of color are always on the go, we carry the strain and trauma of systemic oppression, injustice, and feelings of rejection and being misunderstood within us. Our trauma is like no other. Traumatologist and brain health specialist Dr. Damond T. Holt helps us understand the trauma people of color face:

Black American communities have experienced historical trauma as a result of being enslaved, Jim Crow laws, and ongoing systemic racism, which have contributed to ongoing trauma and health disparities. These health disparities include diabetes, high blood pressure, chronic kidney disorders, to name a few. The effects of historical trauma can be difficult to heal and often require a collective and community-based approach that addresses not only individual symptoms but also the systemic and historical forces that contribute to ongoing trauma and health disparities. This may involve initiatives such as community-based healing programs, cultural revitalization, and education and advocacy efforts to address systemic racism and other forms of oppression.[219]

As one can see, the trauma of people of color doesn't just affect us mentally; it also manifests in physical symptoms that are all too common in the Black church and community. Often in the Black church, many of our congregants who come to the prayer line have the same complaints. Does this mean Christ our King is not a healer? Does this mean they don't have the right amount of faith? It could mean that we aren't educated on the physical manifestations of mental wounds that stem from Black trauma.

The Black Church Serves a Rejected and Misunderstood King

One thing is clear throughout the New Testament: Christ was concerned about the oppressed, ostracized, and rejected. Surely, King Jesus is concerned with the mental health of people of color. Since Christ is concerned, the Black church should be too—especially the clergy.

The Black church must become and remain well-informed about the distrust our parishioners have toward mental health care. It has been estimated that ten percent of Black people believe the U.S. government created AIDS as a concoction to elim-

> The feelings of rejection and being misunderstood are pain and trauma that people of color live with daily, embodied in both our physiology and psychology.

inate African Americans, and another twenty percent could not rule out the possibility.[220] **The feelings of rejection and being misunderstood are pain and trauma that people of color live with daily, embodied in both our physiology and psychology.**

In her conversation with Dr. Obery Hendricks, Williams states:

> I was talking about religion and depression with Obery Hendricks. Obery is a professor at New York Theological Seminary and the immediate past president of Payne Theological Seminary, the oldest African-American seminary… In his view, 'Many of our churches are not really equipped to make a difference [for depressed people in the congregation] because there's no real tradition of looking deep inside yourself, of meditation, contemplation, and introspection. They continue to confuse emotionality with spirituality.'[221]

One must understand that phrases like "I'm blessed and highly favored" don't eradicate years of oppression and trauma embodied in people of color. A "good hot service" in the Black church doesn't erase the low self-worth that people may have brought with them to church. A good sermon from a favorite preacher does not negate the fact that trauma still needs to be addressed. We have to deal with psychological problems psychologically, just as we deal with physical health problems physically. **How can we expect our congregants to come to us about suicidal ideations if we won't take the time to address or stop over-spiritualizing their trauma?** Dr. Poussaint and Dr. Amy Alexander argue, "Significantly, the role of religion is rarely questioned, although it might be relevant that throughout the more than three-hundred-year history of Black people in the United States, Christian African Americans begin as children to absorb the teaching that strife and tribulation here on earth will be redeemed by the sweetness of a heavenly afterlife."[222] Many of our congregants in the Black church have been frustrated by what I call "after-life solutions" to the current realities of discrimination, racism, poor neighborhoods, lack of adequate coping skills, and inequality in education—leaving us in a state of ongoing traumatization.

Poussaint and Alexander further contend, "Many Black churches have for decades preached on the 'sin' of taking one's own life, an archaic outlook that may contribute to the wall of secrecy that continues to prevent African Americans from engaging in open discussions about family members who struggle with depression or self-destructive behaviors."[223] Furthermore, **if we only see our young Black people, for instance, as troublemakers and "gangsters," we are overlooking the fact that the rebellion of our youth in the Black church and Black community is a manifestation of unresolved trauma.**

Poussaint and Alexander posit:

> Missing from the recent limited public discussion of the rise in Black suicide are realistic assessments of the possible motivations for the increase. The proliferation of guns, violence, and drugs, the breakdown of the extended family structure, involvement in the criminal justice system, and a pervasive sense of hopelessness among young people in many Black communities are important but largely overlooked. These factors, combined with a

misguided view held by some young Black males of what constitutes 'respect,' could very well represent a formula that will inevitably lead to more and more Black people bringing their lives to a premature end.[224]

The suicide of rejection and feeling misunderstood is killing our Black men, women, and children daily in more ways than we may realize. Trauma is prevalent in both the Black church and Black community. Many assume that since the post-civil rights era, the trauma of slavery, discrimination, segregation, and racism would have healed by now. However, Holts and Dawson argue:

> The legacy of Black Codes and Jim Crow continues to have a profound impact on Black communities in the United States today. The trauma and pain caused by centuries of segregation and discrimination have left lasting scars on the collective consciousness of Black people and continue to shape their experiences in the present day. When the legal framework of segregation was dismantled, many of the structures and institutions that supported it not only remained in place but, due to the current political climate, are being re-engaged. Black people continue to face discrimination in areas such as housing, education, employment, healthcare, and criminal justice.[225]

The Black church still has Christ as our King but also has trauma as our pain. Nevertheless, trauma does not have to dominate our future, even though it is affecting our present. Christ has provided us with therapists, psychologists, and psychiatrists who can be trusted and are willing to assist people of color. We must face our fears in order to confront our unaddressed trauma. Both clergy and congregants of the Black church must become educated. Why? Because unaddressed trauma is a significant risk factor for suicide.

CHAPTER SEVEN

Black Men On Suicide Watch

"I saw my son's depression, but I didn't
understand depression. I saw he was down,
but I just thought he was moody."
—Les Franklin

It is no secret that the male ego is at the heart of what we do. It has been said that the male ego is fragile. It's also well-known that men define themselves by what they do. As the saying goes, "If you ask a woman who she is, she will tell you how she feels. If you ask a man who he is, he will tell you what he owns, drives, or does for a living." But in a world dominated by white supremacy, police brutality against men of color, racial discrimination, unequal opportunities, and fatherlessness, how does the Black male define himself?

Black men have been craving the success that chattel slavery took away. African American males want to achieve the American dream so much that many have sold drugs, stolen from their own mothers and fathers, and even robbed churches. On July 24, 2022, two young Black men, Juwan Anderson and Say-Quan Pollack, both 23, entered a predominantly Black church, Tomorrow International Ministries in Brooklyn, New York. It was reported that Anderson and Pollack, armed with firearms, robbed members of the church of one million dollars in jewelry.[226]

While robberies are committed across all nationalities and have occurred since biblical times, Black men face harsher consequences than men of other races. Dr. Robinson contends:

> Majorities of both races in America say Black people are treated less fairly than Whites in dealing with the police and by the criminal justice system as a whole. In a 2019 survey, 84% of Black adults said that, in dealing with police, they are generally treated less fairly than Whites; 63% of Whites agreed. Similarly, 87% of Blacks and 61% of Whites said the U.S. criminal justice system treats African Americans less fairly. Negative stereotypes of African Americans as violent criminals have led to the widespread use of race in the creation of law enforcement profiles. Accordingly, to be Black—especially to be a young Black male—means being seen as a suspect.[227]

To address suicide in the Black church, we must deal with the mental health and emotional distress of Black men in both the church and the community. As mentioned earlier, Black women are often filling the church pews to capacity, while many of our Black men are not in church for various reasons—incarceration being at the top of the list. It is no coincidence that Christ made it clear that one of the criteria He will use to judge the "sheep" and "goats" is: "I was in prison and you came to see me" (Matthew 25:36, ESV).

To address suicide in the Black church, we must deal with the mental health and emotional distress of Black men in both the church and the community.

Dr. Tate states, "A large percentage of African American males comprise the U.S. prison population, being imprisoned at a higher rate than Whites. 'African Americans make up 2.7% of the nation's wealth and 40% of the incarceration population; these racial disparities are older than the United States itself.'"[228] Interestingly, Yahweh's first question to the first man, Adam, was, "Where are you?" (Genesis 3:9, ESV). In order for us to address the emotional distress, mental health, and suicidal ideations within the Black church and community, we must ask that same question.

PLACES MEN DON'T CALL HOME

In the 1959 play, *A Raisin in the Sun*, Lena Younger, who plays Walter's mother, has a conversation with Walter (played by Sidney Poitier):

> *Mama: I'm sorry about your liquor store, son. It just wasn't the thing for us to do. That's what I want to tell you about—*
> *Walter: I got to go out, Mama—*
> *Mama: It's dangerous, son.*
> *Walter: What's dangerous?*
> *Mama: When a man goes outside his home to look for peace.*

Additionally, it is my argument that African American men haven't felt at home even before we left home. Tate contends:

> In Willie Lynch's letter to enslavers of this country, he implores his fellow enslavers to 'divide man from his family, and a man from his wife, to break him down psychologically and to show the nigger woman that the male can be easily broken. By doing this, we can see the division between Black families being forcefully engrained within the community—this

operation of assault in grandness during the historical period of slavery in this country.'[229]

Tate further posits, "The atrocities of this mindset were not contained to working days only, but this assault against Black humanity extended even into their church and worship services."[230] It has been the strategy of the slave masters and white supremacists to keep Black males in a low state of status, which psychologically caused low self-esteem and depression in Black men. As quiet as it's kept, this strategy still permeates America today. **African American men struggle to believe they can succeed in the "White man's domain." The plan was to first cause division within a man's home; consequently, this would lead the man to leave his family in search of peace**

African American men struggle to believe they can succeed in the "White man's domain." The plan was to first cause division within a man's home; consequently, this would lead the man to leave his family in search of peace

I THOUGHT I WAS WINNING

Men of color often feel that despite their aspirations, success, and rewards, they are still viewed as three-fifths of a man by White America.

I once heard Bishop T.D. Jakes state in a sermon, You Can Recover From a Fall, "What makes losing bad is when you've gotten used to winning." That profound statement could not have been said any better, especially when it pertains to African American males. **Men of color often feel that despite their aspirations, success, and rewards, they are still viewed as three-fifths of a man by**

White America. In fact, "some researchers have identified the Black man as the invisible man."[231] This leads us to our next subject: the Suicide of Success.

> *26 Samson said to the young man who was leading him by the hand, "Lead me where I can feel the pillars supporting the temple, so I can lean against them." 27 The temple was full of men and women; all the leaders of the Philistines were there, and about three thousand men and women were on the roof watching Samson entertain them. 28 He called out to the LORD, "Lord GOD, please remember me. Strengthen me, God, just once more. With one act of vengeance, let me pay back the Philistines for my two eyes." 29 Samson took hold of the two middle pillars supporting the temple and leaned against them, one on his right hand and the other on his left. 30 Samson said, "Let me die with the Philistines." He pushed with all his might, and the temple fell on the leaders and all the people in it. Those he killed at his death were more than those he had killed in his life. (Judges 16:26-30, CSB)*

Scholars still debate whether Samson truly committed suicide. One must understand, however, that in Jewish culture, they feared Yahweh. When they experienced bouts of depression after traumatic events, they prayed that God would take their life or wished to die (1 Kings 19:1-4; Jonah 4:8). Samson, known for being the strongest man in Scripture and for accomplishing insurmountable feats, still wanted to die despite all his success. It is important to note Samson's death wish and the emotional distress he faced during his life.

The E's of the Suicide of Success

Often, when Samson is discussed, much attention is given to his God-given strength and his weakness for women. However, what is often overlooked is his marriage. Judges 14:20 records that "his wife was given to one of the men who had accompanied him" (CSB). Simply put, Samson's wife married one of the thirty men who attended Samson's party. Other translations specify that it was Samson's best man. This is what I call the espousal issues of Black men. Samson was strong, but he was weak when it came to showing love to his wife.

Many African American men struggle with expressing emotions to their wives. In the Black community, parents often tell their children, "Stop crying before I give you something to cry about." **Parents are also stricter with their sons, not wanting them to become too "soft" or show too much emotion. As a result, by the time young Black men enter relationships, they've been conditioned to keep their emotions to themselves.** While Samson was good at displaying anger, he struggled with another issue: emotions.

If we study closely, Samson's anger towards his wife's betrayal led him to leave her for a few days:

> *1 Later on, during the wheat harvest, Samson took a young goat as a gift and visited his wife. "I want to go to my wife in her room," he said. But her father would not let him enter. 2 "I was sure you hated her," her father said, "so I gave her to one of*

the men who accompanied you. Isn't her younger sister more beautiful than she is? Why not take her instead?" 3 Samson said to them, "This time I will be blameless when I harm the Philistines." 4 So he went out and caught three hundred foxes. He took torches, turned the foxes tail-to-tail, and put a torch between each pair of tails. 5 Then he ignited the torches and released the foxes into the standing grain of the Philistines. He burned the piles of grain and the standing grain, as well as the vineyards and olive groves. (Judges 15:1-5, CSB)

In the passage above, Samson went to visit his wife, but her father made it clear that he thought Samson was divorcing her. Enraged, Samson vented by capturing three hundred foxes, setting them on fire, and letting them destroy the Philistines' harvest. His actions eventually led to him being captured:

6 Then the Philistines asked, "Who did this?" They were told, "It was Samson, the Timnite's son-in-law, because he took Samson's wife and gave her to his companion." So the Philistines went to her and her father and burned them to death. 7 Then Samson told them, "Because you did this, I swear that I won't rest until I have taken vengeance on you." 8 He tore them limb from limb and then went down and stayed in the cave at the rock of Etam. 9 The Philistines went up, camped in Judah, and raided Lehi. 10 So the men of Judah said, "Why have you attacked us?" They replied, "We have come to tie Samson up and pay him back for what he did to us." 11 Then three thousand men of Judah went to the cave at the rock of Etam, and they asked Samson, "Don't you realize that the Philistines rule us? What have you done to us?" "I have done to them what they did to me," he answered. 12 They said to him, "We've come

> *to tie you up and hand you over to the Philistines."*
> *Samson told them, "Swear to me that you yourselves*
> *won't kill me." 13 "No," they said, "we won't kill*
> *you, but we will tie you up securely and hand you*
> *over to them." So they tied him up with two new*
> *ropes and led him away from the rock. 14 When*
> *he came to Lehi, the Philistines came to meet him*
> *shouting. The Spirit of the LORD came powerfully*
> *on him, and the ropes on his arms became like burnt*
> *flax and fell off. (Judges 16:6-14, CSB)*

In this passage, Samson's own people, the men of Judah, betray him and hand him over to the Philistines after interrogating him about burning their crops. Notice that Samson's violent act stemmed from learning that his father-in-law gave his wife to his best man. His feelings of betrayal intertwined with his emotional and espousal issues, leading him to become embittered. To be embittered means to be very angry about the things that happened to you.[232] This was an era without therapists or psychologists, but had Samson received the therapy he desperately needed, his outcomes might have been different.

Neurologist and author Dr. Victor M. Erlich states:

"Samson defends himself against the Philistine vengeance that he should have expected. He finds an old jawbone of an ass, with which he kills another thousand Philistines. All this could be thought of as a kind of mania, but mania is episodic, often shifting back and forth between a variety of intensely driven pursuits and a calm, reasonable, and recognizable personality. Samson is never calm, never himself, never truly a nazir, never a mere womanizer, never a reliable soldier, always an exhibitionist, always in pursuit of the most recent fabrication of his immature executive function. His personality is constant only in that his frontal lobes are reliably unreliable."[233]

Dr. Erlich's assessment of Samson's unresolved anger speaks volumes. **Black males often feel like they can never be themselves, never be calm, and never celebrate their success with-**

out encountering "trauma reminders" of systemic racism. The suicide of success is closely tied to another form of self-destruction: the suicide of impulsivity. Like Samson, many young Black males face dire consequences because of unchecked impulses, which is a lack of self-control—one of the fruits of the Spirit (Galatians 5:22-23).

Cosby and Poussaint contend:

> The need to stop hurting our children and ourselves has been eloquently expressed as a primary concern in Black communities. A non-violent way of life would make Black communities sanctuaries where all felt protected, including the children. To make this happen, Black people have to rein in their anger and recognize that abuse and violence are not part of the solution for the problems we face today.[234]

Samson's unresolved anger, violence, and impulsivity led to toxic coping mechanisms that never healed him. His espousal issues, emotions, and feelings of embitterment ultimately led to entertainment issues. By "entertainment," I mean that Samson coped by sleeping with prostitutes, which eventually brought him down through Delilah:

> *When Delilah realized that he had told her the whole truth, she sent this message to the Philistine leaders: "Come one more time, for he has told me the whole truth." The Philistine leaders came to her and brought the silver with them. Then she let him fall asleep on her lap and called a man to shave off*

Black males often feel like they can never be themselves, never be calm, and never celebrate their success without encountering "trauma reminders" of systemic racism.

the seven braids on his head. In this way, she made him helpless, and his strength left him. Then she cried, "Samson, the Philistines are here!" When he awoke from his sleep, he said, "I will escape as I did before and shake myself free." But he did not know that the LORD had left him. The Philistines seized him, gouged out his eyes, brought him down to Gaza, and bound him with bronze shackles. He was forced to grind grain in the prison. But his hair began to grow back after it had been shaved. (Judges 16:18-22, CSB)

Samson entertained his trauma instead of addressing it. His impulsivity, manifested in uncontrolled anger and forbidden relationships, led to his downfall. By the time he was with Delilah, he was so consumed by pride that he didn't even realize Yahweh had left him. Although his hair grew back, much like Black men who may achieve success, the chains he remained in symbolized the unresolved issues that success alone couldn't fix.

> **Samson entertained his trauma instead of addressing it. His impulsivity, manifested in uncontrolled anger and forbidden relationships, led to his downfall.**

Black Males Ultimate Deadliest Coping Skill

> **Depression in Black males doesn't always look like typical depression.**

Depression in Black males doesn't always look like typical depression, as mentioned in earlier chapters. Some Black men cope with it through substance use, while others turn to sex. Some "work it off" at the gym, and others stay busy to avoid confronting their feelings. However, of all the ways Black males cope with depression, isolation is the go-to for many African American men. As noted earlier in this chapter, Walter's mother warned him of the dangers of seeking peace outside the home. Samson's pain was ignited when, in a moment of anger and impulsivity, he left his wife—only to return and find her married to his best man.

Samson isolates, but he doesn't do it alone. He isolates with random women. In Judges 16, he connects with a prostitute and leaves her as soon as he's done. Clearly, leaving was a coping mechanism for him. But unlike his previous encounters, Samson didn't get to leave Delilah on his own; he was carried away by his enemies. Black males, dealing with unaddressed trauma, high levels of stress, and the burden of protecting the fragile male ego, often act out their mental illness and pain in ways that lead to dire consequences. It's important to note that Samson's public downfall was a manifestation of his private one—his isolation.

The first thing Samson learned from marrying a Philistine woman was that she couldn't be trusted. The second lesson is that he leaves the home when faced with marital conflict. However, not all Black men who isolate are dealing with marital issues. Some also distance themselves from their friends. Bishop T. D. Jakes comments on this sad reality:

> We men need one another. And the sad reality is that most of us aren't in touch with this need because it makes us feel so uncomfortable, so needy, so afraid of being vulnerable and ending up hurt—like being the last one picked at recess for the team—that we bury it and suffer our masculine journeys alone in silence. As we grow up, we grow apart, believing that autonomy is part of masculinity. But the sad truth is we live our lives in solitary confinement that imprisons the masculine soul.[235]

Samson isolates himself through destructive behavior, pride, and impulses, sealing his fate before being imprisoned by his enemies. As strong as he was, Samson kept getting tied up by those who sought to defeat him. Similarly, **Black men, despite the progress made for people of color in the U.S., often find themselves frustrated that their success doesn't heal their internal pain or change white America's view of them.** Even when successful Black men move into suburban areas, they often carry the anxiety of having white neighbors call the police on them.

> Black men, despite the progress made for people of color in the U.S., often find themselves frustrated that their success doesn't heal their internal pain or change white America's view of them.

SUCCESSFUL & ANXIOUS

Radio personality Charlamagne opens up about his anxiety regarding success while living in a white neighborhood:

> Overt racism doesn't slow me down or give me anxiety at all. It's the subtle, passive-aggressive, 'not sure if it's there' racism that gets me stuck in my own head. Once I started making money, one of the first things I did was move into a 'nice' area of Teaneck, New Jersey. What makes it 'nice'? Well, the houses are big. The lawns are manicured. Schools are good. But probably the area's biggest selling point was that there weren't any 'niggers' living in it. Except for me. That's not exactly true. There was plenty of 'niggatry' in my new neighborhood, it was just coming from my white neighbors.[236]

Charlamagne recalls an incident where his white neighbors called the cops on a Black male friend who was waiting for him outside his home:

> As soon as I stepped out my door, I saw two cops had Wax and my boy Shad (who had just pulled up himself) in handcuffs. When one of the cops saw me coming out of my house, he said, 'Do you live here with your parents?' That really threw me for a loop because I was over thirty at that point. Why would he ask me that? 'No,' I replied. 'I live here with my wife and kids, and this is my house. And those are my friends who I invited over. Why are they in handcuffs?' The cop explained that a neighbor had called to report a suspicious man in front of their house. 'Why is he suspicious?' I asked. 'Because he's a Black man in front of his friend's house putting tags on his car in broad daylight?' 'Listen, we're just responding to the call,' replied the cop.[237]

This highlights the chronic anxiety Black males experience, knowing they will eventually be confronted by racial profiling from police, triggered by white neighbors who don't think they belong in a "white" neighborhood. Charlamagne notes that after asking why his friends were in handcuffs, the cops pointed out they had outstanding traffic tickets. Then, his neighbor came running out of his house, shouting, "I knew it! I knew it! What did they have? Guns? Drugs?"[238]

Despite the success of Black men in America, they are not seen as equals by white supremacists.

While the cops let his friends go, Charlamagne—like many other Black men—lives with the anxiety of being discriminated against by law enforcement and in his neighborhood. **Despite the success of Black men in America, they are not seen as equals by white supremacists.** While white society often views Black people as strong, that strength is seen as a threat or only valuable for manual labor. Intellectual strength is rarely acknowledged. Menakem explains:

> The notion of Black fearsomeness and invulnerability requires its mirror image: the fantasy of white fragility. For centuries, white Americans have lived under a strange and contradictory delusion: Black bodies are incredibly strong, frightening, and impervious to pain. They can handle anything short of total destruction. But white bodies are extremely weak and vulnerable, especially to Black bodies. So it's the job of Black bodies to care for white bodies, soothe them, and protect them—particularly from other Black bodies. White bodies have lived with this myth, and allowed it to guide their behavior, for many generations.[239]

This pattern of thought described by Menakem has conditioned people of color to walk on the other side of the street when a white person is approaching. It has also conditioned African Americans to ensure that white people feel comfortable in their presence. Trying to protect white bodies creates embodied trauma for Black people. Menakem adds, "For many African Americans, this collusion becomes second nature—a protective, reflexive response. Just as many white bodies go on alert when they see a Black one in the vicinity. But there is a crucial difference here: the white body tends to shift into self-protection mode."[240]

Additionally, Black physical strength has historically been exploited by white supremacists for cheap labor. Menakem explains how rich white bodies devalued Black people but relied on their strength for labor:

Historically, the myth was most visible on (but not limited to) plantations where enslaved Africans served as cooks, wet nurses, nannies, and victims of sexual exploitation by white plantation owners and their families. We continue to see it just as systemically today—in hospitals, nursing homes, assisted living facilities, and childcare centers, where a high percentage of caregivers are Black. It is also no accident that, in the twenty-first century, large numbers of African Americans work as cooks, private-care nurses, and aides and prostitutes.[241]

It appears that the "suicide of success" correlates strongly with the "suicide of impulse." **When Black men feel that their hard work doesn't earn them the recognition they deserve in a white-dominated society, their impulses may lead to self-destruction, an effort to prove their manhood in comparison to white men.** Dr. Joseph Cooper, a psychologist and sports expert, notes:

> There is a deeply seated pathology that Black males are genetically predisposed to be talented athletes and less gifted in areas outside of sports and entertainment. As with my AAU teams, it is not uncommon for Blacks to make up the majority of football and men's basketball players at big-time colleges, while being a small fraction of the school's overall student enrollment. At the kindergarten through

12th-grade level, Black males are more likely to be celebrated for their athletic prowess and less likely to be selected for gifted and honors classes, let alone be recognized for their performance in these classes.[242]

Interestingly, Samson's enemies, after capturing him from Delilah, wanted him to entertain them, "to make sport of him" (Judges 16:25, KJV). The Hebrew word for "sport" is Śāḥaq (saw-khak'), meaning to laugh in contempt or derision, or simply to entertain. They didn't mind Samson being their entertainment, but they did mind him being the man Yahweh called him to be. This is the frustration of Black men: as long as they conform to societal expectations while denying their skin color, heritage, and identity, they are accepted. Keep in mind that the Philistines wanted Samson to entertain them while he was still in chains.

Grier and Cobbs state:

> The Black boy growing up encounters strange impediments. Schools discourage his ambitions, training for valued skills is not available to him, and when he triumphs in some youthful competition, he receives compromised praise, not the glory he might expect. In time, he comes to see that society has locked arms against him. Rather than help, he can expect opposition to his development, and he lives not in a benign community but in a society that views his growth with hostility.[243]

One can see why Black males are self-destructing at high rates through promiscuity, crime, drugs, and overspending, to name a few. Grier and Cobbs further contend:

> For the Black man, attaining any portion of manhood is an active process. He must pen-

etrate barriers and overcome opposition in order to assume a masculine posture. The inner psychological obstacles to manhood are never as formidable as the impediments woven into American society. By contrast, for the white man in this country, the rudiments of manhood are settled at birth by the possession of a penis and white skin.[244]

If the Black church doesn't take the plight of Black males seriously by educating themselves on Black suicide, we will lose more of our men.

No Tears to Get Rid Of

One thing that is clear in Samson's narrative is that we see no expression of tears. His wife is given to his best man, and he does not cry. He sets the foxes' tails on fire and allows them to run through the crops of his enemies (Judges 15:4-5). He dealt with his pain by doing to his enemies what they did to him (Judges 15:11). The suicide of impulse is what causes one to react out of pain in ways that are self-destructive. Like Samson, our men of color have been reacting, not responding, to discrimination, racism, and lack of equality in America.

Author and expert in Emotional Stability Training, Jason Wilson, discusses how unaddressed pain in Black fathers affects Black sons:

> Throughout their young lives, boys are taught to withstand the strain of holding in their tears, suppressing them until it hurts. Eventually, they grow into men who fear appearing vulnerable—a fate no self-respecting man can live with. The majority of fathers I've worked with

over the years truly want the best for their sons. However, because of unresolved anger associated with how they were mistreated by their own dads, they are hindered from expressing the love they longed for. As men, we have to cease fathering from our wounds and seek healing from the trauma we've received so our sons can be loved comprehensively.[245]

One of the sad realities is that our Black males have mastered displaying anger but struggle with the pride and fear of releasing tears. Christ our King, who came to earth as God in the flesh, demonstrated for us the significance of a man's tears. The Bible highlights three moments in Jesus' life where He cries.

> *41 When He approached Jerusalem, He saw the city and wept over it, 42 saying, "If you had known on this day, even you, the conditions for peace! But now they have been hidden from your eyes. (Luke 19:41-42, NASB)*

> *35 Jesus wept. (John 11:35, NASB)*

> *7 In the days of His humanity, He offered up both prayers and pleas with loud crying and tears to the One able to save Him from death, and He was heard because of His devout behavior. (Hebrews 5:7. NASB)*

Christ, who is King of the Kingdom of God, our Lord and Savior, the Mediator between God and men, took time out of His busy schedule to display tears. **The Black church must teach our Black males that to be Christ-like is to cry sometimes.** However, the question is: will the Black Church be ready to handle a man's tears? Wilson further argues:

Every boy needs a crew; every man needs camaraderie and a safe place to not only express his emotions but also release them, venting his cares to someone who really cares. Sadly, a man's concerns are often heard as complaining, just as a dog's bark is annoying when no one sees trouble. Both warnings are rarely heeded before "the thief" breaks in and steals, kills, and destroys everything, even the dog. As men, we must take care of ourselves by truthfully expressing ourselves with other men we can trust. No matter your age group, transparency will set us free.[246]

UNADDRESSED ANGER REMOVES BLACK MALES FROM THEIR ADDRESS

The rage of Black males is a rage that goes beyond marital problems, a stock market crash, or even a traffic ticket. Our rage stems from the chronic racial trauma of wrestling with the suicide of success and the suicide of impulse. Author and Pastor, Bishop George D. McKinney, expounds on the rage of Black males:

Anger is born from injustice. It flares when I am treated as less than I believe myself to be. That was probably true of Frederick Douglass as well. He rightly believed himself to be human, with the heart, soul, and just claim to freedom of any other man. But then he and his grandmother were treated with the cruelty one might reserve for beasts, for insects. Rage flared within him… That is the kind of rage I am focusing on here, not the momentary outbursts of anger we all experience and quickly deal with. I am referring to the kind of rage that begins as early as infancy and is borne from injustices and violations that we continue to experience long after the events that caused them are forgotten, enshrined in dark, seething memory.[247]

The rage of Black males can be so strong that it consistently removes us from our own address. Suicidal tendencies in Black males are often expressed through rage that has not been addressed in therapy. Many young African American males are expressing anger as early as kindergarten. The irony is, this child is diagnosed with ADHD and placed in special education classes—moved from the address of quality education.

The rage of Black males can be so strong that it consistently removes us from our own address. Suicidal tendencies in Black males are often expressed through rage that has not been addressed in therapy.

There are Black males who come from abusive homes and are now abusing their girlfriends and wives. Interestingly, some of these Black males are clergy, deacons, and serve in the Black church while beating their wives. In no way should we condone domestic violence. However, we must also not condone unaddressed trauma in the Black church. Unaddressed rage is removing fathers from their homes and sending them to serve long prison sentences.

There are good fathers who struggle with rage while trying to be the father they never had.

Last but certainly not least, we must recognize that despite the negative images of African American males acting out rage through gang violence, drive-by shootings, and street fights, not all of the rage comes from "gangstas" and "thugs." **There are good fathers who struggle with rage while trying to be the father they never had.** There are fathers doing their very best to raise their children in the church to be respectful citizens, yet they are stressed and filled with rage, knowing their children—especially boys—are at a higher risk of being killed by the police.

This is why I call this the suicide of success. The suicide of success for Black males trying to strive, succeed, and leave a legacy for their families is often tied to premature death in a country where racism, discrimination, and segregation are still alive and well. Highly acclaimed civil rights lawyer, advocate, and legal scholar Michelle Alexander argues:

> The fact that some African Americans have experienced great success in recent years does not mean that something akin to a racial caste system no longer exists. No caste system in the United States has ever governed all Black people; there have always been 'free Blacks' and Black success stories, even during slavery and Jim Crow. The superlative nature of individual Black achievement today in formerly white domains is a good indicator that the old Jim Crow is dead, but it does not necessarily mean the end of racial caste. If history is any guide, it may simply have taken a different form.[248]

The suicide of success in Black males is strongly linked to the suicide of impulse. When Black males give up hope in America, it increases the likelihood of them committing suicide. In Dr. Alton R. Kirk's book Black Suicide, Ain, who lost her father to the suicide of success, states:

> In 2002, Dad was one of 31 people who completed suicide in the District of Columbia (DC) that year. He hung himself with an extension

cord at the age of 57. I was two months shy of 30. Thankfully, I did not find him. He was burdened by many things, past and present, in his last year of life. He ended up abandoning routine activities and withdrawing from regular contact with me and my older brother. He surrounded himself with music and books that reinforced his negative feelings—especially those centering on the plight of Black men. He died believing that he wouldn't achieve the life he wanted.[249]

The suicide of success ignites the suicide of impulse due to people of color feeling like all their hard work does not pay off. We saw this in the administration of the 44th President, Barack Hussein Obama, who served from 2009 to 2017. On January 6, 2021, when a "heavily armed mob of supporters of outgoing President Donald Trump stormed the U.S. Capitol,"[250] questions arose about how this large group of white supremacists was able to bypass Capitol security with minimal effort. Black America already knew the answer: racism.

CEO of Black Star Network and former CNN contributor Roland Martin states:

What we have seen in American history is that Black success is always followed by White backlash. Whether triggered by the fear of Blacks in positions of power or the fear that Black folks would take White Americans' jobs, this backlash has been the consistent pattern in this country.[251]

These retraumatizing events that Blacks continue to witness affect and infiltrate every fiber of our being. When Holt and Dawson spoke with Dr. Warren Stewart, Sr., senior Pastor of First Institutional Baptist Church in Phoenix, Arizona, Dr. Stewart postulates:

> Trauma is stressful and traumatic. This trauma is not only post-traumatic but also present and traumatic. As Black Americans, we live traumatic lives on a daily basis—even in our homes, while shopping, worshipping, and entertaining ourselves. This is Post and Present Traumatic Stress Disorder. Trauma from living in a world of systemic racism, trauma from living in a world of continuous discrimination, where Black Americans have to be twice as good and still not be recognized as equal.[252]

Black men are losing their patience. Black men in the Black church are losing their patience as well. Black men with degrees are running out of patience. Black men with extravagant homes are running out of patience. Black men with no criminal record are running out of patience. Black males who are faithful to their wives are running out of patience. Our Black males' mental health and suicidality must be taken seriously before they act on their suicidal thoughts.

CHAPTER EIGHT

Meeting the Suicidal Where They Are

"That's the problem with being the strong
one. No one offers you a hand."
—Anonymous

Before King Jesus ascended into heaven, He gave His disciples the command to "Go into all the world and preach the gospel to all creation" (Mark 16:15, LSB). The question we must ask ourselves is, what gospel was Christ referring to? There are an immense amount of teachings infiltrating pulpits across the globe, leading congregants to believe they are being taught the true gospel. However, the apostle Paul warned, "But even if we, or an angel from heaven, should proclaim to you a gospel contrary to the gospel we have proclaimed to you, let him be accursed!" (Galatians 1:8, LSB).

The only gospel that was preached by the King of kings was what Christ called "this gospel of the Kingdom" (Matthew 24:14). The Greek word for gospel is euangelion (yoo-ang-ghel'-ee-on), which means good tidings or good news. What was the good news that brought Jesus Christ, our King, out of eternity and caused Him to step into time? What was this gospel of the Kingdom?

Andrews et al. state, "The gospel of the Kingdom is the realm of God's active goodness in forming us in Christ as we follow Him. The Kingdom of God is grand, majestic, and full of beauty. We come to understand the Kingdom by repenting and simply becoming apprentices of Jesus in His Kingdom."[253]

This was the gospel that Christ wanted proclaimed throughout all creation, regardless of race, color, ethnicity, or gender. Listen to what Christ said: *"The Spirit of the Lord is on me, because He has anointed me to proclaim good news to the poor. He has sent me to proclaim freedom for the prisoners and recovery of sight for the blind, to set the oppressed free, to proclaim the year of the Lord's favor" (Luke 4:18-19, NIV).* Christ sought to bring the gospel of the Kingdom to those the Pharisees considered outsiders, the least important in their eyes.

Dr. Obery M. Hendricks, Jr., remarks:

"In this passage, Luke's Jesus leaves no doubt as to the radicality of His calling. First, He heralded good news to the poor (ptochois, the Greek word for "poor" here, indicates a collective or class identity). That is, He announced that the reason for His ministry was to struggle for radical change in the circumstances and the institutions that kept people downtrodden and impoverished."[254]

The gospel that Christ preached was about the Kingdom of God being a present reality for those whom society looked down upon. King Jesus came to give us "the right to become children of God" (John 1:12, ESV). The apostle Paul reminds us that in Christ, there is "neither Jew nor Greek, slave nor free, male and female, for you are all one in Christ Jesus" (Galatians 3:28, ESV). Entrance into the Kingdom of God is predicated on our obedience to this gospel of the Kingdom. The issue, however, is that many are too hurt and angry to obey the gospel that came to set them free.

CHURCH HURT IN THE BLACK CHURCH

Many have walked away from the Black church in the Black community, feeling that it has become irrelevant and unresponsive to the plight of people of color. Some millennials believe the Black church has turned into an entertainment business, profiting off Black people's emotions. It's still debated today, and widely believed among many people of color, that the Bible is the "white man's" tool for brainwashing us. A plethora of podcasts are dedicated to urging Black people to leave the church and recognize that we are gods. However, we know this contradicts Scripture, for there is "one Lord, one faith, one baptism" (Ephesians 4:5, ESV).

Yet, many in the Black community, including some within the Black church, aren't open to hearing that message. They're fed up with a church they feel has been manipulated by the "Slavery Bible," which they believe has kept people of color suppressed. Nevertheless, Jemar Tisby, president of The Witness, a Black Christian Collective that addresses race, religion, politics, and culture, states, "The church has not always and uniformly been complicit with racism. The same Bible that racists misused to support slavery and segregation is the one abolitionists and civil rights activists rightly used to animate their resistance."[255]

Despite the many challenges the Black church has faced and overcome, many of our millennials have given up on it. Dr. Mason writes:

> A central population of African American culture has been to confront the wounds and scars of African American people, and historically the Black church has labored greatly in this effort. However, a new generation does not know the bridge that has brought us over troubled waters in the past. They see the church as dated and impotent and are exploring cults, sects, and new ideologies. They turn to the internet for answers the church once provided. Today's African American church must engage the work of urban apologetics and learn to answer the barbershop questions people are

asking while introducing the illuminating and transcendent truth of the gospel.[256]

The Black church must understand that people of color are leaving and turning to other sects and cults that stimulate their minds and address their mental health. **While the Black church is well-versed in fighting for civil rights, we must now fight against the ideologies that are targeting the minds of our people.** This leads us to what I've coined the "suicide of religion."

> **While the Black church is well-versed in fighting for civil rights, we must now fight against the ideologies that are targeting the minds of our people.**

THE SUICIDE OF RELIGION

4 The Philistines gathered and camped at Shunem. So Saul gathered all Israel, and they camped at Gilboa. 5 When Saul saw the Philistine camp, he was afraid and his heart pounded. 6 He inquired of the LORD, but the LORD did not answer him in dreams or by the Urim or by the prophets. 7 Saul then said to his servants, "Find me a woman who is a medium, so I can go and consult her." His servants replied, "There is a woman at En-dor who is a medium." 8 Saul disguised himself by putting on different clothes and set out with two of his men. They came to the woman at night, and Saul said, "Consult a spirit for me. Bring up for me the one I tell you." 9 But the woman said to him, "You surely know what Saul has done, how he has cut off the mediums and spiritists from the land. Why are you setting a trap for me to get me killed?" (1 Samuel 28:4-7, CSB).

The Philistines fought against Israel, and Israel's men fled from them and were killed on Mount Gilboa. 2 The Philistines pursued Saul and his sons and killed his sons, Jonathan, Abinadab, and Malchishua. 3 When the battle intensified against Saul, the archers found him and severely wounded him. 4 Then Saul said to his armor-bearer, "Draw your sword and run me through with it, or these uncircumcised men will come and run me through and torture me!" But his armor-bearer would not do it because he was terrified. Then Saul took his sword and fell on it. (1 Samuel 31:1-4, CSB).

In both passages cited above, we are introduced to the suicide of Saul, the first king of Israel. He was not the king God desired for Israel; however, the people were insistent on being like the other nations (1 Samuel 8). Despite God's warning about what Saul would do to them, Israel's insecurity drove them to irrationally believe they needed a human king when Yahweh was already their sole King of kings. Saul disobeyed God during his reign, and as a result, the Spirit of God departed from him forever. Although Saul remained king, God was no longer with him, which is why he ultimately sought the advice of a witch.

Saul's suicide didn't begin when he took his own life; it began when he rejected the Word of the Lord. The prophet Samuel tells him, "Because you have rejected the word of the LORD, He has rejected you as king" (1 Samuel 15:23b, CSB). From that moment, Saul was never right within. Without God's Spirit, Saul exhibited signs of mental illness, such as anxiety and loss of appetite. Consider how the Bible describes the day before Saul's suicide:

20 Immediately, Saul fell flat on the ground. He was terrified by Samuel's words and was also weak because he had not eaten anything all day and all night. 21 The woman came over to Saul, and she saw that he was terrified and said to him, "Look, your servant has obeyed you. I took my life in my hands and did what you told me to do. 22 Now please listen to your servant. Let me set some food in front of you. Eat and it will give you strength so you can go on your way." 23 He refused, saying, "I won't eat. (1 Samuel 28:20-23a, CSB)

Interestingly enough, Saul was told by the prophet Samuel that he was going to die in battle; however, Saul was unaware that his death would come through suicide. Disobedience to the commands of the LORD resulted in Saul taking his own life. This is what I call the "suicide of religion." If we are going to address suicide among Kingdom believers in the Black church, we must acknowledge that many in the Black community have either left the church or joined non-Christian religions. Three of the major religions that many former Christians of color are now affiliated with include Islam, Hebrew Israelites, and Jehovah's Witnesses.

According to Pew Research, "Protestantism has long dominated the Black American religious landscape, and still does. The survey shows that two-thirds of Black Americans (66%) are Protestant, 6% are Catholic, and 3% identify with other Christian faiths – mostly Jehovah's Witnesses. Another 3% belong to non-Christian faiths, the most common of which is Islam."[257] The research further revealed that "about one-in-five Black Americans (21%) are not affiliated with any religion and instead identify as atheist, agnostic, or 'nothing in particular,' and this phenomenon is increasing by generation."[258]

One reason the Hebrew Israelites are successful in recruiting people of color is that many Black individuals feel they have no identity in the United States. Mason describes how the Hebrew Israelites, particularly the 1West groups, attempt to recruit people of color on the streets:

> West groups will typically establish a presence in high-foot traffic areas and ask Black passersby, 'What's your nationality?' Their goal in doing this is to wake up the 'Negro' to the truth that Blacks, Hispanics, and Native Americans are really the original Israelites

spoken of in the Bible. The question, 'What's your nationality?' will typically produce a variety of answers. Most Black people in the western hemisphere don't know where their ancestors were from in Africa, and many African Americans struggle to call themselves exclusively American.[259]

It must be understood that the Black church has been a place of identity for people of color who experience imposter syndrome outside its walls. At the same time, many African Americans are leaving the Black church and joining other religions, cults, or movements that offer a sense of identity and self-esteem. The suicide of religion for people of color involves losing faith in Christ and what His Word says we are.

For years, the hip-hop culture and Black Muslims have been vocal in rejecting the portrayal of Jesus as a blue-eyed, blond-haired figure. Many believe that Christianity is a white man's philosophy projected onto people of African descent to manipulate them during slavery. However, a vast majority of Black people do not see Jesus Christ as part of a white man's religion. Historically, the Black church has provided people of color with a sense of self-worth.

Civil rights activist and clergy member Reverend Al Sharpton reflects on the self-esteem boost that the Black church offered to people of African descent:

> Looking back at it now, I can see how we Black folks had created our own world, our own meeting place. Washington Temple, and places like it, were safe, and in retrospect, I now see that it was the only place that Black people of that generation could be somebody. Think of all those butlers and bellhops and janitors and domestic workers and delivery boys— they had to bow down all week long. But on

Sunday morning at Washington Temple, they were chairman of the Deacon Board, they were trustees, they ran the building fund, they were Madam Chairwoman of the Mother's Board, they were the choir director. People that everybody ignored all week could stand up and speak their thoughts or perform before thousands of their peers.[260]

It is vitally important that the Black church reaches out to the Black community, just as Christ sought the lost sheep (Luke 15:1-7), searching for those who left the church because they lost faith in Christ due to the ongoing battle against racism, which many see as a losing fight. I argue that when African Americans leave the Black church after years of service and dedication, they leave behind a significant part of their mental health. This leads us to the next issue: the suicide of inferiority.

It is vitally important that the Black church reaches out to the Black community, just as Christ sought the lost sheep.

It's noteworthy that when Samuel confronted Saul about his disobedience, Saul was more concerned with preserving his ego than with restoring his relationship with Israel's true King, Yahweh. He said to Samuel, "I have sinned. Please honor me now before the elders of my people and before Israel" (1 Samuel 15:30a, CSB). As we see in this statement, Saul cared more about his reputation than about his relationship with God.

Saul's insecurity was evident even before he became king. When Samuel informed him that he would be Israel's next king, Saul responded, "But am I not a Benjamite, from the smallest tribe of Israel, and is not my clan the least of all the clans of the tribe of Benjamin? Why do you say such a thing to me?" (1 Samuel 9:21, NIV). Even Yahweh remarked on Saul's insecurity:

"Although you were once small in your own eyes, did you not become the head of the tribes of Israel?" (1 Samuel 15:17, NIV).

The suicide of insecurity runs rampant in the mental health of people of color. Dr. Degruy observes the effects of systemic racism on African Americans in relation to Post-Traumatic Slave Syndrome (PTSS):

> Society contributes to the formation of PTSS and vacant esteem in a number of ways: through its laws, institutions, and policies, as well as through the media. African Americans have been and continue to be disproportionately represented in our penal institutions. African Americans often live in neighborhoods where schools are functionally segregated and lack adequate revenue to sustain them. In African American communities, banks charge higher interest rates on homes and auto loans, and it is more difficult for African Americans to get small business loans.[261]

Every time a Black person is turned down for a home loan, it strikes a blow to their self-worth, especially when they know their skin color played a significant role in the bank's decision. When people of color look around their poverty-stricken neighborhoods, they feel the pain and inadequacy of living in such conditions. The suicide of insecurity is reinforced daily by the systemic racism that Black people face—whether it's through their environment, education system, workplace, or economic conditions.

One thing we've learned, and others already know, is that insecurity is contagious.

The Suicide of Company

If insecurity is contagious, the suicide of insecurity is as well. I strongly believe, from both a clinical and biblical perspective, that the suicide of insecurity leads to my final suicide: the suicide of company. Now, let's revisit the suicide of Saul and pay attention to the scenario in greater detail:

> *1 Now the Philistines fought against Israel; the Israelites fled before them, and many fell dead on Mount Gilboa. 2 The Philistines were in hot pursuit of Saul and his sons, and they killed his sons Jonathan, Abinadab and Malki-Shua. 3 The fighting grew fierce around Saul, and when the archers overtook him, they wounded him critically.4 Saul said to his armor-bearer, "Draw your sword and run me through, or these uncircumcised fellows will come and run me through and abuse me."But his armor-bearer was terrified and would not do it; so Saul took his own sword and fell on it. 5 When the armor-bearer saw that Saul was dead, he too fell on his sword and died with him. 6 So Saul and his three sons and his armor-bearer and all his men died together that same day. (1 Samuel 31:1-6, NIV)*

In the above passage, Saul is ready to follow through and commit suicide. After Saul takes his life, his armor-bearer commits suicide as well. The last verse shows us that Saul did not die alone. Saul's last recorded words in the passage are a request for his armor-bearer to kill him. He did not ask his armor-bearer to commit suicide; he asked him to commit homicide. When I refer to the suicide of company, I am alluding to the daily accumulating rate of homicide committed in the Black community. I will use the remainder of this chapter to elaborate on this tragedy and concern by discussing two major categories of the suicide of company.

Homicide is the New Suicide in the Black Community

Dr. Degruy, in her book Post Traumatic Slave Syndrome, delves into a scene where she witnessed two teenage boys getting into an altercation. She narrates that while the argument wasn't serious in the beginning, it ended with one of them pointing a gun in the other's face. The boy with the gun pointed at him responded, "Do you think I'm afraid to die?[262] I ain't afraid to die." What intrigued me about this story was that when the gun was held up to this Black teenager's head, Degruy states, "The gun jammed. Dominic did not run. Dominic did not attack."[263]

While Degruy reports that Dominic lived, the question remains: why wasn't he afraid to die? Degruy argues:

> Most people regarded this event as an attempted murder when, in fact, they witnessed another suicide attempt by a young Black man. Too many young Black men are looking to die, and while there is little glory in putting a bullet in your own head, there is much glory in being killed in a shootout with rival gang members. These are desperate young men, believing that there is no hope for the future. They don't think or care about their lives a year from now, let alone five, ten, or fifteen. Few of them expect to live past their early twenties.[264]

We have to ask ourselves: why aren't Black lives valued by other African Americans in our country?

Cosby and Poussaint contend, "Homicide and suicide have a lot in common. They are both forms of violence in which guns are often the weapon of choice. We can't allow this."[265] Many who lack the courage to take their own lives will provoke someone else to do it. Unfortunately, in the Black community, we are provoking each other. What does what is going on in the Black community have to do with the Black church, one might ask? Remember, Degruy points out that it is the lack of hope that lies at the substratum of Black homicide and suicide.

This innocent killing, or taking of the lives of other Blacks, is known as "Black-on-Black crime." The statistics for Blacks killing Blacks in 2020 are as follows:[266]

- Whites killing Blacks –2%
- Police killing whites—3%
- Whites killing whites—16%
- Blacks killing whites—81%
- Police killing blacks—1%
- Blacks killing Blacks—97%

This is the sad reality we live in. We have been oppressed, discriminated against, and vilified to the extent that we have turned on each other. Additionally, not all homicides involve guns or other weapons. Some homicides are what is known as "murder of the mouth." There are many in the Black community—and even within the Black church—who struggle with the second category of the suicide of company: jealousy.

> One of the signs that our people are depressed and unhappy is the self-hate that manifests in how we talk about each other.

As stated earlier in this chapter, depression in Blacks has distinct features that don't always resemble traditional depression. This is why it's vital for the Black church to get educated on mental health, especially suicidality. **One of the signs that our people are depressed and unhappy is the self-hate that manifests in how we talk about each other.** Reality shows display people of color fighting each other, Black celebrities castigating one another, and dark-skinned African Americans talking down to lighter-skinned African Americans. The self-hate among us is real, to the point where we don't congratulate each other for our successes or support Black-owned businesses.

In poverty-stricken inner-city neighborhoods where people of color reside, one can look around and see the ways in which jealousy leads to self-destruction. Psychology shows us that jealousy not only destroys but also self-destructs. In urban neighborhoods with low-income housing, one can see the graffiti on houses, abandoned buildings used as crack houses, beer cans on the streets, and empty chip bags flying through the wind. Additionally, one can't help but notice the sirens of police cars rushing through traffic in broad daylight to respond to incidents of Blacks shooting other Blacks, gang violence, and domestic violence calls.

In some ways, it appears that African Americans are conditioned to accept this as the norm to the extent that we can walk past this daily in our neighborhoods without getting involved. This is the suicide of company. **When people of color give up on ourselves, seeing other Black people succeed breeds contempt and jealousy.** Anne Gold posits, "Although low self-esteem is not categorized as a mental health condition in itself, there are clear links between the way we feel about ourselves and our overall mental and emotional well-being."[267]

Furthermore, this self-hatred plays a critical role in Blacks robbing each other, stealing each other's cars, and raping our own people. While theft is theft, murder is murder, and rape is rape in any ethnicity, culture, or race across the globe, this dissertation focuses primarily on the plight of the Black church and the Black community.

HOMICIDE IS NOT OUTRUNNING SUICIDE AMONG US

While homicide is an issue in the Black community, which the Black church is also a part of, it does not appear to surpass the number of suicide statistics for people of color. Poussaint and Alexander contend:

> While the rate of serious crime in the country has dropped, an average of 85 suicides were taking place each day. As a cause of death in the United States and a public health problem, the total number of suicides had, by the late 1990s, topped that of homicides, at about 31,000 deaths per year compared with about 21,000 homicides.[268]

Suicide and homicide are cousins but certainly not twins. This is an issue that Black churches hear about weekly, watch on the news, and might scroll past on social media, but they fail to address it from the pulpit. We have to break our silence. In the Black church, one of the predominant sayings is, "changing a generation." However, how can we change a generation whose mental health we ignore? How can we change a generation if we don't take seriously that there might be neglected youth in the congregation who could be contemplating suicide?

While we have nice youth Sunday services, are we having youth mental health services? Authors Rose Jackson-Beavers and Jermine D. Alberty state:

> Unfortunately, young people who experience depression may have a desire to kill them-

selves. One study found that among Black youth, 3.2% reported some suicidal thoughts in the past year; 1.4% reported attempting suicide (Joe et al., 2009). This may seem like a small number. However, suicide is the third leading cause of death among Black youth (Lincoln et al., 2012). Researchers have also found that suicide rates have doubled for Black children while declining for white children. They were surprised by their own results. This is the first recorded data in history for which Black suicide rates surpass those of other races.[269]

Furthermore, **we cannot save our millennials and Gen Z'ers without first addressing our mental health.** Remember, Christ made it clear that those who are not sick don't need a physician (Luke 5:31). I would also argue that those who aren't struggling with their mental health or battling suicidal ideations don't need a therapist.

> We cannot save our millennials and Gen Z'ers without first addressing our mental health.

Emotional Distress & Suicide Attempts

"Do not harm yourself, for we are all here."
—The Apostle Paul

As stated in chapter one of this book, I did not know how to help the woman in my church after she mentioned she was contemplating suicide. Everything she confided in me prior to that phone call made no mention of suicide. She primarily talked about her marriage, depression, and low self-esteem. Now that I am trained in suicidality, I can see, in retrospect, that she was experiencing a combination of mental health challenges and emotional distress. I will use this chapter to discuss the differences between mental illness and emotional distress, terms that are often used interchangeably but are not synonymous. I will also examine a pivotal moment in the life of Jesus Christ, our Eternal King, to see how He dealt with emotional distress.

LATEST RESEARCH PERSPECTIVE ON SUICIDE

There is an insurmountable amount of myths about suicide that have germinated cognitive distortions around the topic. One of those myths is that everyone who commits suicide has a mental illness or is struggling with depression. Nonetheless, leading expert in suicide prevention, Dr. Craig J. Bryan, proves otherwise:

> I want to take a moment and acknowledge that some individuals who attempt suicide have a preexisting, albeit undiagnosed, mental illness because they never sought treatment. For these individuals, the suicide attempt often brings them into contact with the mental healthcare system for the first time, at which point a previously undiagnosed mental illness is recognized and diagnosed. I'm not arguing that these individuals did not have a mental illness to begin with. Rather, I'm arguing that some who attempt suicide or die by suicide—perhaps more than we have traditionally assumed—probably do not have a mental illness at all. This latter group might be experiencing significant emotional distress, and this emotional distress may have pushed them toward suicidal behavior, but emotional distress is not the same thing as mental illness.[270]

Dr. Bryan's research is pivotal in assisting African American clergy, the Black church, and the Black community in understanding suicidality. **What stops many of us from going to therapy is the fear of being diagnosed as "mentally ill." It is vital to understand that emotional distress is not the same as mental illness.** We will now turn to the Word of God and scrutinize the emotional distress that Christ, our King, experienced when He came to earth in His human body.

What stops many of us from going to therapy is the fear of being diagnosed as "mentally ill." It is vital to understand that emotional distress is not the same as mental illness.

Emotional Distress in the Garden of Gethsemane

32 They came to a place named Gethsemane; and He said to His disciples, 'Sit here until I have prayed.' 33 And He took with Him Peter, James, and John, and began to be very distressed and troubled. 34 And He said to them, 'My soul is deeply grieved, to the point of death; remain here and keep watch.' 35 And He went a little beyond them, and fell to the ground and began praying that if it were possible, the hour might pass Him by. 36 And He was saying, 'Abba! Father! All things are possible for You; remove this cup from Me; yet not what I will, but what You will.' 37 And He came and found them sleeping, and said to Peter, 'Simon, are you asleep? Could you not keep watch for one hour? 38 Keep watching and praying, so that you will not come into temptation; the spirit is willing, but the flesh is weak.' 39 And again He went away and prayed, saying the same words. 40 And again He came and found them sleeping, for their eyes were heavy; and they did not know what to say in reply to Him. 41 And He came the third time, and said to them, 'Are you still sleeping and resting? That is enough. The hour has come; behold, the Son of Man is being betrayed into the hands of sinners. 42 Get up, let's go; behold, the one who is betraying Me is near!' (Mark 14:32-42, NASB)

In the above passage, our Lord Jesus Christ is getting close to fulfilling His mission of destroying the works of Satan by dying on the cross (1 John 3:8). While it is a Kingdom truth that Jesus Christ is God, He appeared in a human body to die. While in a human body, Christ experienced what it is like to be us. The writer of Hebrews points out that:

> *"7 In the days of His humanity, He offered up both prayers and pleas with loud crying and tears to the One able to save Him from death, and He was heard because of His devout behavior. 8 Although He was a Son, He learned obedience from the things which He suffered. 9 And having been perfected, He became the source of eternal salvation for all those who obey Him, 10 being designated by God as High Priest according to the order of Melchizedek." (Hebrews 5:7-10, NASB)*

It is clear that Christ knew what it felt like to be under emotional distress. In fact, the Word of God makes it clear that Christ can sympathize with our moments of weakness and distress (Hebrews 4:15). The Garden of Gethsemane shows us, through the life of Christ our King, how to cope with emotional stress. We will examine some crucial points from a Christian counseling and psychology perspective while remaining true to the inerrancy of Scripture:

The first principle we can learn from Jesus' emotional distress is the importance of the right atmosphere. Christ chose to come to the Garden of Gethsemane. **Many who struggle with emotional distress believe they can't vent or be themselves.** Their homes no longer feel like gardens but warzones. During the COVID-19 pandemic and quarantine, the domestic violence rate increased. Surprisingly to many, men were being emotionally abused during the quarantine as well. According to journalist Sarah Fielding:

> One caller to a domestic violence hotline reported that her husband threatened to throw her out into the street if she coughed. Another reported

they had been strangled by their partner but feared going to the hospital because of the threat of coronavirus. An immunocompromised man from Pennsylvania called in after his emotionally abusive girlfriend began hiding cleaning supplies and hand sanitizer from him.[271]

The Black church is the place that people of color have trusted in the past as their Garden of Gethsemane, but presently it is seen as a jungle of the wild. Dr. Joshua L. Mitchell comments on the reality of the perspectives of Black millennials as it pertains to the Black church:

> Many Black millennials have had some connection with the Christian church—either by being reared in the life of a congregation or by living with grandparents or loved ones who proclaimed faith in Christ. They've also been exposed to the negative aspects of the church, with scandals and shortcomings of congregations becoming all-too-frequent launching pads for blog posts, Twitter wars, and television series. As a result, long before they darken the doors of a local place of worship, many Black millennials have preconceived notions of the Christian church that the church must contend with.[272]

Many African Americans are distrustful of the Black church and feel like it is no longer a safe place to share secrets, emotional distress, or suicidal ideations. Professor and licensed clinical mental

Many African Americans are distrustful of the Black church and feel like it is no longer a safe place to share secrets, emotional distress, or suicidal ideations.

health counselor (LCMHC) Allashia Smith-Harris states, "From the beginning of the church in America, we were the beacon of hope, the salvation from slavery, the 'escape' from brutality to the truthful reality of trust in Christ. The Black church has been known to be a place of safety, a place of refuge, a place of rehabilitation. It has been known as 'The Hospital for the Saints.'"[273] It is vital that the Black church goes back to being a Garden of Gethsemane for our emotional distress.

Next, Christ shows us that there are those in the body of Christ we can trust. While Christ had twelve disciples, He knew which ones to call on for His supportive network. The Scriptures state, "And He took with Him Peter, James, and John, and began to be very distressed and troubled. And He said to them, 'My soul is deeply grieved, to the point of death; remain here and keep watch'" (Mark 14:33-34, NASB). While there are a plethora of those who have experienced "church hurt" by some in the body of Christ, we can learn from this pivotal moment in the life of Jesus Christ that there will always be someone or a handful of those we can still trust.

Third, this passage teaches us the importance of community. Christ, who is God Himself, shows us that we should not experience high levels of acute stress and emotional distress alone. The church must develop a "suicide community" for those who have contemplated suicide in the past, made a suicide attempt, and are experiencing high levels of emotional distress. The sad reality is that there is a vast majority of congregants in the Black church who are living all alone inside the church.

Another vital lesson we learn in the Garden of Gethsemane is the courage to be vulnerable by telling the truth. Christ told His disciples, "My soul is deeply grieved, to the point of death; remain here and keep watch" (Mark 14:34, NASB). Christ is God, and Jesus our King is the Christ. King Jesus could have said, "I have a reputation to protect. I can't let my disciples see Me like this. I am God in the flesh." However, Paul already made it clear that Christ "although He existed in the form of God, did not consider equality with God something to be grasped, but emptied Himself, taking the form of a servant, becoming like a man" (Philippians 2:6-7, HCSB).

Christ did not preoccupy Himself with insecure thoughts of being seen as weak. They already knew who the King of kings was. Christ is not weak; however, He was experiencing emotional distress. Additionally, what is interesting is that Christ knew His disciples could not help Him, but Christ was our perfect example, according to 1 Peter 2:21. It takes courage for the Black community to verbalize their emotional distress to the Black church. Verbalizing our pain and emotional distress brings healing.

Campbell contends, as she cites Dr. Dan Siegel:

> Earlier we spoke about Dr. Dan Siegel and the principle he coined: name it to tame it. This phrase reflects his neurological research, which found that when we feel distressing emotions, the right side of our brain releases distress signals. When we put words to the pain we're experiencing, the left side of the brain releases calming signals to the right side of our brain, soothing its distress. When we put words to the pain we've endured, it makes those experiences less painful.[274]

There are many in the Black church who feel as if they cannot go to other members in the congregation or confide in their pastor, although they have been told in the past, "You can come talk to me about anything." Others are skeptical of confiding in the Black church because they might have grown up in that church and know the gossipy culture that discusses everyone's business in the kitchen, back of the church, or church parking lot.

Now keep in mind, Christ did not trust His disciples. The Bible is clear: "But Jesus would not entrust Himself to them, for He knew all people" (John 2:24, NIV). The question we must ask ourselves is why Christ would confide in men who loved Him but whom He did not trust. Emotional distress needs an outlet and someone to talk to. Holding emotional distress inside for long periods can lead to suicidal ideations. Psychiatrist Dr. Edward M. Hallowell remarks:

> Never worry alone. This maxim was taught to me when I was in my psychiatric training. When you share a worry, the worry almost always diminishes. You often find solutions to a problem when you talk it out, and the mere fact of putting it into words takes it out of the threatening realm of the imagination and into some concrete, manageable form.[275]

Jesus Christ understood the importance of community. For people of color, community has always been a staple. The Black church has been the "go-to" spot when white churches, which provoked the birth of the AME (African Methodist Episcopal) Church and other Black reformations, did not want to worship with us. Nikole Hannah-Jones remarked:

> The Black church has not only been a forum for righteous anger. Forged out of slavery, it was also a place of protection and practicality. For many decades it was one of the few places Black people could gather for educational purposes, to arrange mutual aid groups, or to form political organizations. As a result, it has always been a target. As an independent institution operating free of white control and oversight, the Black church had inherent revolutionary potential that often made it an object of white fear and anger.[276]

Jones goes on to highlight the sad reality of Black churches that were burned due to racial hatred. She states, "After Michael Brown was killed in Ferguson, Missouri, in 2014, the pastor of

Flood Christian Church repeatedly called out police brutality. One week after Brown's father was baptized at the church, the building was burned to the ground."[277] Thus, one could see why it is vital for the Black church to stick together, considering that eleven o'clock on Sunday morning continues to be the most segregated hour in the divided states of America.

One of Satan's chief tactics, which continues to work very well to this day, is division. The apostle James reminds us, "But if you have bitter envy and selfish ambition in your heart, don't boast and deny the truth. Such wisdom does not come down from above but is earthly, unspiritual, demonic. For where there is envy and selfish ambition, there is disorder and every evil practice" (James 3:14-16, CSB). **When the enemy can incite the Black church to turn against one another, when we are already dealing with external division, it can increase emotional distress and suicidality.**

Lastly, King Jesus continued to talk through His emotional distress. Christ states, "Then He came and found them sleeping. He said to Peter, 'Simon, are you sleeping? Couldn't you stay awake one hour? Stay awake and pray so that you won't enter into temptation. The spirit is willing, but the flesh is weak'" (Mark 14:37-38, CSB). Due to the "You got to be strong" mentality that exists within the Black community, which we don't leave in the car when we step inside the Black church, we struggle to communicate the emotional distress that we are really experiencing.

Hunt contends, "Stay connected with others. If you felt lonely prior to the attempt, it may be one of the reasons that contributed to your suicidal thoughts. Connect with people and strive to keep in touch. Fight off loneliness and allow other people to remind you of why you matter and why life is worth living."[278] What often frustrates many who muster up the courage to share their feelings of hopelessness and helplessness is feeling misunderstood. We must remember that being swift to hear and slow to speak (James 1:19) is pivotal when assisting those in our congregations who verbalize their thoughts of emotional distress, overwhelming anxiety, and major depressive symptoms. Why? The wrong response could discourage them, making it our last conversation.

Sleepy Clergy

Despite Christ asking for His disciples to stay awake, they continued to sleep. Interestingly enough, the Word of God points out that they were sleeping: "When He got up from prayer and came to the disciples, He found them sleeping, exhausted from their grief" (Luke 22:45, CSB). The disciples were able to stay awake when Christ fed the five thousand, walked on water, and even woke Jesus up when He fell asleep. However, the moment that Christ needed them, they went right back to sleep. The Scriptures clearly point out that their sleep was a symptom of exhaustion from grief.

One of the reasons why many clergy aren't responding to the phone calls of their parishioners is due to their secret exhaustion and grief. Yes, preachers get tired too. Pastor, professor, and author Dr. Lewis Brogdon posits:

"The issue of clergy suicide is far more pervasive and complex than most news articles suggest. It speaks to entrenched problems of brokenness and dysfunctional congregations, unrealistic clergy demands, lack of adequate preparation for the rigors of ministry, and insufficient support for clergy and their families. Broken congregational systems and models of ministry replicate the same outcome. To our collective dismay, that is exactly what we are seeing—more suicides."[279]

One of the reasons for clergy suicide, besides mental health, emotional distress, and church obligations, is the exposure of sins. With social media and screenshots of clergy in sexual acts with both the same and opposite sex, it is crucial to ask ourselves what is going on with Black clergy mentally. Brogdon contends:

> These critics believe that many pastors lead double lives and, instead of facing the truth and consequences of their actions, opt to kill themselves. Granted, the number of clergy suicides that involve some form of misconduct is too high and lends itself to the insinuation that the two phenomena are linked. Yet, not all clergy who commit suicide are involved in misconduct. Therefore, another question arises: what is driving alarming levels of misconduct, where a contributing factor is the threat of facing the consequences of that misconduct? It is certainly more complex than just assigning blame to these circumstances.[280]

The Black church must remain cognizant of the fact that when Black clergy, even those exposed for sexual sins or other misconduct, commit suicide, the congregations they pastored are affected as well. Brogdon further argues, "Pastoral suicide traumatizes congregations and forces family members to grieve publicly before the world as news outlets pour into town to report the story. Who helps them process the grief they experience, and who cares about these congregations in the aftermath?"[281] When Black clergy take their mental health and emotional distress seriously, we can truly save souls.

The Black church must remain cognizant of the fact that when Black clergy, even those exposed for sexual sins or other misconduct, commit suicide, the congregations they pastored are affected as well.

Emotional Distress & Suicide Attempts in the Bible

We will now direct our attention to understanding how emotional distress correlates with suicide attempts. In the therapeutic field, there are a plethora of interventions to assist those with thoughts of suicidal ideation, such as Crisis Response Planning (CRP), Cognitive Behavioral Therapy for Suicide Prevention (CBT-SP), Dialectical Behavioral Therapy (DBT), safety planning, and the Columbia-Suicide Severity Rating Scale (C-SSRS). The question is, how educated is the Black church on these methods? One does not have to be a psychologist or licensed therapist to learn these treatment modalities or understand how they are implemented.

Dr. Bryan states,

> All of these suicide-focused interventions—DBT, CBT-SP, and CRP—aim to change how a person makes decisions within the context of intense emotional distress and uncertainty about the future. DBT, CBT-SP, and CRP focus on teaching individuals how to respond to stressful situations in a more balanced and less extreme manner, thereby helping them adopt a safer decision-making style and stick with successful methods, even when they occasionally do not work.[282]

In the above citation, it is vital to note that the key features of emotional distress, as they relate to suicidal ideation and attempts, are decision-making and uncertainty about the future. While Christ told us not to worry about tomorrow (Matthew 6:34), the individual facing emotional distress is more focused on the heat of the moment. **When emotional distress is high, impulsivity can also increase, leading to a suicide attempt.** Contrary to popular belief, many who survived a suicide attempt were not preoccupied with suicidal ideation. They were experiencing what Bryan calls the "tipping points".

Bryan posits:

> Individuals who died by suicide often seemed to be doing reasonably well right up until the moment they attempted suicide, as if they had crossed over some sort of threshold or tipping point. Many (though not all) of my patients often said that they didn't necessarily feel any better or any worse than they had the day before (or the week or the month before that). On the contrary, they often explained that they 'just couldn't take it anymore.'[283]

While there is a principle commonly known in psychological studies as the 90% statistic (which posits that ninety percent of those who die by suicide had a mental illness[284]), this percentage has become questionable according to Bryan. He points out that, in many cases, there was a dearth of evidence to support this probability.[285] Thus, it is vital to understand that some of our parishioners who experienced a survived suicide attempt probably were not experiencing depression or suicidal thoughts in the days leading up to the attempt.

A SUICIDAL ATTEMPT IN THE BIBLE

To further accentuate Bryan's findings, from a Biblical perspective, we will scrutinize a case in the Word of God involving a suicide attempt:

> *25 About midnight, Paul and Silas were praying and singing hymns to God, and the rest of the prisoners were listening to them. 26 Suddenly a great earthquake occurred, shaking the foundations of*

the prison. Immediately all the doors flew open, and the bonds of all the prisoners came loose. 27 When the jailer woke up and saw the doors of the prison standing open, he drew his sword and was about to kill himself because he assumed the prisoners had escaped. 28 But Paul called out loudly, "Do not harm yourself, for we are all here!" 29 Calling for lights, the jailer rushed in and fell down trembling at the feet of Paul and Silas. 30 Then he brought them outside and asked, "Sirs, what must I do to be saved?" 31 They replied, "Believe in the Lord Jesus, and you will be saved, you and your house-hold." 32 Then they spoke the word of the Lord to him, along with all those who were in his house. 33 At that hour of the night, he took them and washed their wounds; then he and all his family were baptized right away. 34 The jailer brought them into his house and set food before them, and he rejoiced greatly that he had come to believe in God, together with his entire household. (Acts 16:25-34, NET)

In the above passage, the apostle Paul and Silas encounter a man who is about to attempt suicide. Remember, this was a time when suicide prevention phone numbers were not available, psychiatrists and licensed counselors were unheard of, and there were no associations like the American Association of Suicidality to provide psychoeducation. This was the 1st century. Now let's consider the fact that the narrative does not say anywhere that this nameless man was depressed. We do not read about any problems in his marriage or childhood wounds of the past. His suicide attempt was based on witnessing a miracle in a jail cell.

In verse 27, we see: "When the jailer woke up and saw the doors of the prison standing open, he drew his sword and was about to kill himself because he assumed the prisoners had escaped" (Acts 16:27, NET). Thus, prior to Paul and Silas being delivered from prison, the man had nothing to contemplate suicide over. However, we do have one discovery:

> *22 The crowd joined the attack against them, and the magistrates tore the clothes off Paul and Silas and ordered them to be beaten with rods. 23 After they had beaten them severely, they threw them into prison and commanded the jailer to guard them securely. 24 Receiving such orders, he threw them in the inner cell and fastened their feet in the stocks. (Acts 16:22-24, NET)*

Paul and Silas were turning the world upside down with the gospel of the Kingdom and demonstration of the Kingdom through miracles, signs, and wonders. The magistrates wanted to ensure that Paul and Silas would never cast out another demon again. To secure this, they commanded the jailer to guard them securely. Dr. Dave Miller states:

> Roused from his sleep, the jailer saw that the prison doors had been jarred open, causing him to fear that the prisoners had, in fact, escaped. Consequently, he 'drew his sword and was about to kill himself' (Acts 16:27). Why? True, allowing prisoners to escape is bad, but why would it merit committing suicide? The historical evidence indicates that Roman jailers were required to take personal responsibility for the prisoners committed to them. This charge was serious. Negligence in this matter meant inevitable death—perhaps even by slow, painful torture.[286]

Rather than face the torture of a slow death, the jailer was ready to act on his impulses. If this incident took place in the 21st century, how would the Black church respond to the jailer?

Lessons from Jailor on Addressing Suicide Attempts

It is helpful to note that for a long time after the first century, churches did not comment on or address suicide. Augustine, however, was one of the first to speak on the subject, as was Thomas Aquinas.[287] The Council of Arles became the first church conclave to condemn suicide in 452 A.D.[288] Dr. H. Norman Wright states, "During the Middle Ages, civil law began to follow the teaching of the Church and prohibited suicide. Desecration of the corpse of a suicide became standard practice. Bodies of suicide victims were dragged into the street... In England, the last body to be dragged through the streets and buried at a crossroads was in 1823."[289]

The Black church can benefit from learning how to support those who have verbalized suicidal attempts and ideations. Acts 16 provides us with helpful tips on what to do when one of our parishioners is going through a suicide crisis. First, we must recognize that the gospel is for the suicidal as well. In Acts 16, we find an interesting passage:

> *6 They went through the region of Phrygia and Galatia, having been prevented by the Holy Spirit from speaking the message in the province of Asia. 7 When they came to Mysia, they attempted to go into Bithynia, but the Spirit of Jesus did not allow them to do this, 8 so they passed through Mysia and went down to Troas. 9 A vision appeared to Paul during the night: A Macedonian man was standing there urging him, "Come over to Macedonia and help us!" 10 After Paul saw the vision, we*

> *attempted immediately to go over to Macedonia,*
> *concluding that God had called us to proclaim the*
> *good news to them. (Acts 16:6-10, NET)*

Paul wanted to go through other cities, but the Holy Spirit told him no twice. The Holy Spirit decided to give Paul a vision of where He wanted him to go. That vision included a Macedonian man asking Paul for help. In the same chapter, Paul ministers to a woman named Lydia (Acts 16:14-15), but she was not the man in the vision. Paul and Silas also cast the demon out of a young girl who practiced divination (Acts 16:16-18), but she was not the man in the vision. Acts 16 has only one man who gets ministered to, and that was the jailer.

> **The Black church must take mental health seriously because to minister the gospel of the Kingdom is to minister the Word of God to a troubled mind.**

The Black church must take mental health seriously because to minister the gospel of the Kingdom is to minister the Word of God to a troubled mind. We aren't providing holistic ministry if we ignore those members in the church who do not seem like themselves lately. Remember, the prince of darkness (Satan) is after the minds of those who have already been transformed by the renewing of their minds (Romans 12:2). Many in the Black church are dancing and shouting on Sunday morning but crying themselves to sleep Sunday night. When clergy are not educated in mental health and suicidality, we are missing a gargantuan part of ministry.

Next, this passage teaches us the importance of community. Paul and Silas could have run out of jail after King Jesus sent the earthquake that set them free; however, they chose to provide a supportive network for this man, who was their enemy. His emotional distress mattered more to Paul and Silas than holding a grudge the enemy probably wanted them to hold. The Black church is filled with a multiplicity of services, from extravagant conferences to lavish Holy Convocations. We are known to host plays, skate nights for the youth, and even fashion shows.

Nevertheless, real fellowship may not happen when the music is playing but when the single mother in the church's emotional distress is addressed by the pastors. **Real fellowship is when congregants get together to take the depressed teenager out to eat and provide a safe space for them to discuss what is really bothering them.** Real fellowship is when we hear what each other is going through and do more than say, "You're in my prayers." Notice Paul and Silas prayed and sang praises unto God before they were miraculously delivered from jail. However, the Scriptures are clear that they did not pray for the man when they saw he was about to kill himself.

Furthermore, notice Paul and Silas did not say to the man, "Hey! Don't kill yourself. You will go to hell if you do." No, they provided empathy. Paul said, "Don't harm yourself! We are all here!" (Acts 16:28, NIV)! If community is a staple of the Black church through slavery, Jim Crow, police brutality, and other injustices faced by Blacks, it is certainly a staple for addressing emotional distress and suicide attempts. When Christ rose from the dead, Thomas was not there with the other disciples (John 20:24). However, Christ showed up eight days later for Thomas. Kingdom ministry shows up.

Third, Paul and Silas listened to him. The Black church must develop a sensitive ear for those who are on the verge of taking their lives. When Paul and Silas listened to the man, they realized he had some questions. Interestingly, this suicidal man had a religious question: "Sirs, what must I do to be saved?" (Acts 16:30, NET). Paul and Silas did not preach to him before he asked this powerful question. Keep in mind, this man was not suicidal prior to this event. The Bible does not specify that. What we can imply from a psycho-theological lens is that he was dealing with a crisis of emotional distress, which Dr. Bryan points out in his book, *Rethinking Suicide.*

Fourth, Paul and Silas met him where he was. They simply answered his question: "Believe in the Lord Jesus, and you will be saved—you and your household" (Acts 16:31, NIV). Many in our congregations, particularly in the Black church, have questions about their suicidal ideations that they feel too ashamed to bring to the church. The fear of being told, "You don't have enough faith," "You aren't praying enough," or "You know you're going to hell if you keep thinking like that" looms large. Paul did not give him a discourse on eschatology (the study of last things) or a dissertation on overcoming strongholds. Paul and Silas met this man where he was.

Paul and Silas did not have a therapist to refer the man to, nor did they have knowledge of a safety plan. However, they used what they knew to assist him. Thankfully, the man brought up the topic of salvation, which opened a door to discuss religion. It's vital for Christian therapists and clergy who are licensed Christian therapists to remember that counseling is not the same as preaching.

Scholar, author, and founder of Christian Bible Institute & Seminary, Dr. Tony V. Lewis states:

> Christian counseling involves a balance between grace and truth. This means active listening on the one hand and challenging on the other. Active listening must be given the premier place. Active listening is the most important skill an effective counselor must learn, as it builds a relational background for challenging, and challenging would be the second most important, as it encourages the person to choose life.[290]

Paul did not make himself the star in this man's life. The objective of licensed Christian therapists should be to point the individual to Christ. Christian psychologist Dr. Mark R. McMinn contends:

> Effective Christian counselors recognize that counseling relationships often point clients toward a healthier view of God. The counseling relationship is helpful when it displays aspects of God's character; it's harmful when it becomes a means of personal power, grandiosity, or self-gratification. When prayer draws more attention to the counselor than to God, it misses the mark.[291]

Lastly, Paul and Silas went to the man's house. This is pivotal. We must remember that the Black community is a part of the Black church. Although that praying mother's son does not attend church, the Black church should prioritize reaching the family members of our congregants, especially if we are aware of their emotional distress and mental health struggles. When we visit the gospels, we see Christ our King in the house of Mary and Martha (Luke 10:38-42); Simon (Luke 7:37); and Zacchaeus (Luke 19:5-10). Christ spoke about leaving the ninety-nine in the wilderness and searching for the one who was lost (Luke 15:1-4).

We must be concerned about the young millennial who stopped singing in the choir. We should be concerned about the young man who left the church and never came back. We must be concerned about those who mention they're "tired"— not assuming they only mean physically. Paul and Silas show us the importance of ministering to those who struggle with suicide attempts and how to minister to them. Even after someone has survived a suicide attempt, we must continue to check on them. Contrary to popular belief, not everyone in the Black church has "a feeling that everything will be alright."

Looking at the Jailor from a Counseling Psychology Professional Lens

Bryan's research in suicidality has demonstrated what works and does not work in the counseling profession regarding the prevention of suicide attempts. Bryan outlines three models that attempt to reduce suicidality, of which only one model has proven effective today. The first model is the risk factor model. This model focuses on understanding suicidal thoughts and behaviors by identifying and describing their correlates.[292] Bryan and Rudd contend:

> The risk factor model does not necessarily propose any specific underlying process or cause for suicidal behavior, but rather assumes that it is the accumulation of multiple risk factors that contribute to suicidal thoughts and behaviors. Treatment informed by this model aims to reduce the risk factors under the assumption that doing so will reduce the incidence and/or severity of suicidal thoughts and behaviors.[293]

Unfortunately, this model has had relatively minimal impact on suicide prevention.[294] Next is the *psychiatric syndrome model.* According to Bryan and Rudd, "From this perspective, suicidal thoughts and behaviors are described and organized according to observable characteristics and surface features of the behaviors (e.g., method, lethality, and intent), similar to the syndromal classification schemes commonly used in mental health and medical professions."[295] Similarly, this method has also proven to have little effect.

Bryan and Rudd further posit, "Although the psychiatric syndromal model has predominated in our clinical understanding of suicide for decades and is the perspective from which most clinicians approach the treatment of suicidal patients, accumulating evidence has failed to support the effectiveness of this conceptual framework."[296] Lastly, there is the *functional model*. This model posits that suicidal thoughts and behaviors have little to do with psychiatric illness but are instead shaped by how psychological processes are experienced.[297] This last model takes into account three factors: the individual's personal history, the immediate environment, and the behavioral responses.[298] Thankfully, this model has proven to be the most effective.

To give further credence to the effectiveness of the functional model, we will utilize the jailor's story in Acts 16. If a suicide prevention team met the jailor, they would examine risk factors such as the proximity of weapons (the jailor pulled out his sword to kill himself). Thus, in this case, reducing the risk means removing all weapons from his home. If a psychiatrist were to meet with the jailor, they would look for symptoms of depression, PTSD, or GAD (Generalized Anxiety Disorder).

However, the functional model bypasses the first two models and approaches the jailor with different objectives in mind. The functional model wants to assess the jailor's emotional regulation: what made him think suicide was the way out (cognitive)? What emotions was he experiencing (emotional)? What actions did the jailor take after waking up and finding Paul and Silas free from their Roman chains (behavior)? This is vital information for all psychiatrists, psychologists, licensed counselors, and Christian counselors to keep in mind when dealing with those facing suicidality in the Black church and Black community.

In short, **we must remember that emotional distress is not the**

> **We must remember that emotional distress is not the same as mental illness.**

same as mental illness. The jailor was not battling depression, paranoid schizophrenia, or bipolar disorder; he was facing a crisis of emotional distress. Put another way, this was a suicide attempt—not suicidal ideations. Bryan and Rudd argue, "Suicide attempts are a much closer approximation to suicide death than suicide ideation or psychiatric diagnosis."[299]

As for Black clergy, we would need to keep a close eye on the jailor if he were a member of the Black church today. Although he survived the suicide attempt, he was still employed at the same job where the emotional distress took place. Black individuals live in the same America that has a history of injustice causing racial, historical, and complex trauma. Licensed professional counselor (LPC) and author Dr. LaVerne Hanes Collins, who specializes in racial trauma, states:

> Whether your ancestors arrived in 1620 on a slave ship, or you arrived in 2020 on a jumbo jet, discrimination awaited anyone with dark skin.[300]

SUICIDE AND TERMINOLOGY

One of the major problems in reducing the suicide rate is the issue of suicide language. Bryan argues that a lack of consistent language hampers progress and comprehension of research regarding populations with a history of and/or increased risk for self-directed violence (SDV).[301] Furthermore, Bryan provides us with a list of key terms that will assist us in understanding the various degrees of suicidality:[302]

- Self-Directed Violence: Behavior that is self-directed and deliberately results in injury or the potential for injury to oneself.
- Suicidal Intent: There is past or present evidence (implicit or explicit) that an individual wishes to die,

means to kill himself/herself, and understands the probable consequences of his/her actions or potential actions. Suicidal intent can be determined retrospectively and in the absence of suicidal behavior.

- Preparatory Behavior: Acts of preparation toward engaging in self-directed violence, but before the potential for injury has begun. This entails anything beyond a verbalization or thought, such as assembling a method (e.g., purchasing a gun) or preparing for one's death by suicide (e.g., writing a suicide note or giving away prized possessions).

- Physical Injury: A bodily lesion resulting from acute overexposure to energy (this can be mechanical, thermal, electrical, chemical, or radiant) interacting with the body in amounts or rates that exceed the threshold of physiological tolerance (e.g., bodily harm due to suffocation, poisoning or overdose, lacerations, gunshot wounds, etc.).

- Interrupted by Self or Others: An individual takes steps to injure themselves but is stopped by themselves or another person prior to fatal injury. The interruption can happen at any time.

- Suicide Attempt: A non-fatal self-inflicted potentially injurious behavior with any intent to die as a result of the behavior.

- Suicide: Death caused by self-inflicted injurious behavior with any intent to die as a result of the behavior.

These terms fall under two groups: thoughts and behaviors.[303] Thoughts are classified as either "non-suicidal self-directed violence ideation" or "suicidal ideation," while behaviors are grouped as either "preparatory," "non-suicidal self-directed violence," "undermined self-directed violence," or "suicidal self-directed violence."[304]

THERAPY THAT WORKS

Despite the myriad of therapeutic interventions in counseling and psychology, Cognitive Behavioral Therapy (CBT) has stood the test of time. While Dialectical Behavior Therapy (DBT), which began in the late 1980s by Dr. Marsha M. Linehan, was developed because she believed CBT was not effective in treating patients with suicidal ideations, DBT treatment can be "resource-intensive, time-consuming, and difficult to learn."[305] Thus, Brief Cognitive Behavioral Therapy (BCBT) seeks to achieve what DBT has done in a more condensed manner.

Bryan argues that BCBT is the next course of action in the development and reworking of the CBT model, which has proven to be beneficial for clinical researchers over the course of several decades.[306] Clergy in the Black church, African American therapists, and the Black community can benefit from learning BCBT. It's also vital for both Christian and non-Christian counselors to learn BCBT. Why? The American Association of Suicidology reported that approximately ninety percent of mental health professionals confess to having an actively suicidal client on their caseload, while fewer than half obtained training on suicidality in graduate school, medical school, or professional training.[307]

CHAPTER TEN

The Data Results

*"It is not those who are well who need a
doctor, but those who are sick."*
—*King Jesus*

This chapter will assist in understanding the methods used in this research to corroborate its dependability and reliability. The goal of this research was to highlight the importance and urgency for the Black church to address the taboo topic of suicide within its congregations. Another purpose of this research design is to provide answers as to why Black clergy aren't addressing suicide within the Black church and to gain insight into their theological views as well.

RESEARCH METHODOLOGY

In addition to the relevant literature review, a mixed methods research design was utilized. The diversified methods used in data collection for this research included qualitative data through questionnaires, gathering the thoughts of the Black church on the effectiveness of their awareness of suicide, their level of comfort in discussing mental health, and their concerns and recommendations for the Black Church. Additionally, a qualitative method involving a questionnaire for clergy regarding their theological views on suicide awareness, or the lack thereof, and strategic planning for their churches on a local, national, and international level was used. Qualitative methods also included interviews with licensed mental health professionals who are Black and attend a Black church.

PARTICIPANTS

Volunteers who were invited to participate in this research were members of the Black Church, eighteen years of age and older. Participants who were seventeen years of age or younger were disqualified from the research. Age, race/ethnicity, and gender were the demographics selected by the participants. Criteria for participation included adults in the Black church who experienced suicidal ideations, those free from suicidal ideations for at least one year or more, and friends and family of those who died by suicide. Active clergy, church leaders, as well as Black mental health professionals in the Black church participated in this study.

INSTRUMENTATION

Questionnaire 1: The *Suicide Education Among Clergy Questionnaire* (n=10) was used to interview and gather the perspectives of clergy from denominational and independent Black churches. The questionnaire was designed by the researcher and reviewed by their dissertation academic advisor and a licensed mental health therapist.

Questionnaire 2: The *Suicide Prevention Education in the Black Church Questionnaire* (n=24) was used to interview and gather information from congregants in various denominational and nondenominational settings of the Black church. This interview provided a qualitative analysis to identify the plight of the uncommunicated mental health issues of the parishioners of the Black church. The questionnaire was designed by the researcher and reviewed by their dissertation academic advisor and a licensed mental health therapist.

Questionnaire 3: The *Suicide Survey for the Black Church Members* (n=28) was used to assess the level of satisfaction or dissatisfaction among congregants regarding the past and present strategic planning or lack thereof concerning suicide awareness and prevention. The survey was designed by the researcher and reviewed by their dissertation academic advisor and a licensed mental health therapist.

Interviews were conducted with licensed mental health professionals (n=4) who attend the Black church.

Data Collection

The data for this research was collected from samples of the following: congregants of the Black church; selected pastors and clergy with at least three years of ministerial experience within the Black church; licensed mental health therapists and psychologists who are members of the Black church; family members of at-risk youth in the Black church; and adults in the Black church at risk of suicide who have been free of suicidal ideations and attempts for at least one year. The survey and questionnaires were emailed to ten churches and their pastors who participated, along with several licensed mental health professionals.

Data Analysis

A mixed methods design was utilized for data collection for this pre-intervention research study. The data collected was organized and analyzed by themes, patterns, slippages, and silences. The *Suicide Education Among Clergy Questionnaire* qualitative interview data identified the need for pastors and clergy to break the silence and seriously address the importance of suicide awareness in the Black church, and to contemplate plans for incorporating suicide psychoeducation into their church calendar. The researcher reviewed the questionnaire responses to count and compare the number of educated clergy members versus those who were not fully trained, with percentages computed from the numbers acquired.

The *Suicide Prevention Education in the Black Church Questionnaire* was a qualitative design that highlighted the needs of the congregants in the Black Church who are suffering in silence while remaining committed to their church. The researcher reviewed the questionnaire responses to count and balance the percentage of suicide-related ministry practices in the church and those without them, with percentages computed from the numbers acquired. The *Suicide Survey for the Black Church Members* was a quantitative design utilized to analyze the satisfaction level of congregants regarding the Black church's implementation of strategies to promote suicide awareness and provide psychoeducation from a Christian perspective.

GENERALIZABILITY

While this research primarily focused on suicide among Blacks within the Black church, suicide also exists in predominantly white churches and among other ethnicities. This work aims to highlight the critical importance of addressing the mental health needs of Blacks in the Black church, who live in a re-traumatizing society that often treats people of color as lesser. Anyone repeating this study would greatly benefit from the insights and recommendations of the Black church community. The voice of the Black Church, which has been a cornerstone in the Black community, appears to be declining in influence regarding mental health, particularly suicide awareness and prevention. The goal of this research is to give Black church members struggling with suicidal ideation a platform to voice their experiences and recommendations, countering the efforts to silence the Black voice.

RESULTS

Suicide Education Among Clergy Questionnaire

Data Overview

The dataset includes responses from clergy members about their experiences and practices related to mental health and suicide prevention. Key areas analyzed include the frequency of psychoeducation, certification in suicide prevention, the importance of the suicide topic, belief in Christian psychology, the impact of theological views on suicide awareness, interactions with congregants about suicidal ideations, addressing suicide from the pulpit, personal experiences with suicidal ideations, age, and gender. The respondents (n=10) ranged in age from 29 to 64 years, with a mean age of approximately 42 years. Seven (7) clergy participants identified as male.

Quantitative Analysis

Frequency of Psychoeducation

Clergy members were asked how often they engage in psychoeducation regarding suicide. The responses varied, with half of the respondents frequently engaging in such education. Specifically, 50% reported doing so often, 30% not often, and 20% never engaging in psychoeducation on suicide (Figure 1).

Figure 1. This pie graph illustrates responses to the question, "How often do you keep yourself abreast of psychoeducation regarding suicide?" (n=10).

Certification in Suicide Prevention

When asked about their certification in suicide prevention, the responses were evenly split. Half of the clergy were certified in suicide prevention, while the other half were not.

Importance of Suicide Topic

Clergy members rated the importance of the topic of suicide on a scale from 1 to 10. The majority, 80%, rated it as highly important (10), with the remaining ratings being 8 (10%) and 6 (10%).

Belief in Christian Psychology

All respondents indicated a belief in Christian psychology, underscoring a unified approach towards integrating faith with mental health practices.

Impact of Theological Views on Suicide Awareness

The responses indicated that theological views significantly impact the emphasis on suicide awareness within their ministries for a minority of the respondents. Specifically, 30% stated that their theological views affected their emphasis on suicide awareness, while 70% reported no impact.

Interactions with Congregants Regarding Suicidal Ideations

Half of the clergy reported that they had been approached by congregants with suicidal thoughts, highlighting the need for clergy to be equipped to handle such situations.

Addressing Suicide from the Pulpit

A significant number of clergy members had not addressed suicide from the pulpit. Specifically, 60% reported never addressing the issue publicly, while 40% had done so (Figure 2).

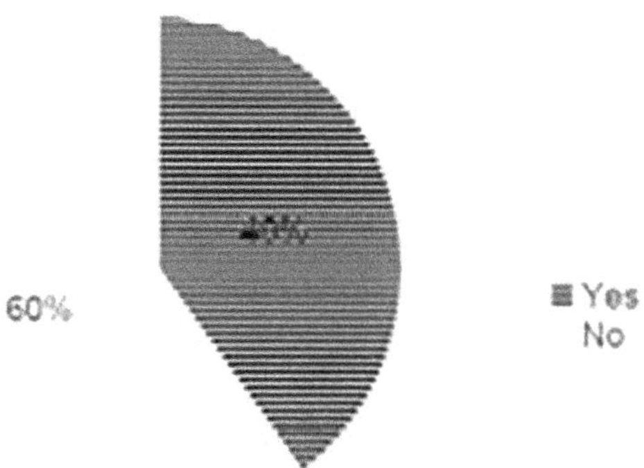

Figure 2. This pie graph illustrates responses to the question, "Have you ever been asked to address this issue from the pulpit as well as other avenues within your reach?" (n=10).

Personal Experiences with Suicidal Ideations

Regarding personal experiences with suicidal ideations, 40% of the clergy reported having struggled with such thoughts, 50% had not, and 10% did not provide a response.

Qualitative Analysis

Common Themes

Education and Awareness: There is a significant emphasis on the importance of psychoeducation regarding suicide among clergy. However, the engagement levels vary, with some regularly updating themselves and others less so.

Certification: The mixed responses regarding certification highlight a need for more formal training and certification in suicide prevention among clergy members.

Importance of Suicide Topic: The topic of suicide is deemed highly important by most respondents, reflecting a recognition of its critical significance in their pastoral roles.

Belief in Christian Psychology: All respondents expressed belief in Christian psychology, indicating a strong inclination towards integrating spiritual and psychological approaches to mental health.

Theological Views: While theological views influence the emphasis on suicide awareness for some, the majority do not find their theological perspectives affecting their focus on this issue.

Interaction with Congregants: Many clergy members have been approached by congregants with suicidal ideations, suggesting a significant need for resources and support mechanisms.

Personal Experience: Several respondents have personal experiences with suicidal ideations, underscoring the importance of mental health support for clergy themselves.

The analysis reveals a multifaceted landscape in which clergy members navigate their roles in suicide prevention and mental health support. The varied levels of certification and engagement in psychoeducation indicate areas where further training and resources are required. The high importance placed on the topic of suicide suggests a recognition of its significance, yet the impact of theological views and the reluctance to address the issue publicly point to potential barriers in effectively integrating mental health support within church activities.

Recommendations

This questionnaire has illustrated a detailed perspective from the responses from clergy regarding their engagement with suicide education and mental health. The findings underscore the need for ongoing education, certification, and the integration of mental health support within church ministries. By addressing these areas, the church can play a pivotal role in supporting the mental well-being of its congregants and clergy alike. The following recommendations arose from the analysis:

1. **Increase Certification and Training**: Encourage more clergy to get certified in suicide prevention to better support their congregants.
2. **Promote Regular Psychoeducation**. Foster a culture of continuous learning and awareness regarding mental health and suicide within the church community.
3. **Normalize Mental Health Discussions**: Create safe spaces for open dialogues about mental health and suicide without stigma.
4. **Utilize Professional Resources**: Involve mental health professionals in church activities and provide congregants with access to counseling services.
5. **Support for Clergy**: Provide support systems for clergy who may also struggle with mental health issues, ensuring they have the resources to seek help.

The recommendations emphasize the need for churches to be proactive in addressing mental health issues, fostering open dialogue, reducing stigma, involving professionals, and providing comprehensive support to congregants. These steps can significantly contribute to better mental health outcomes within the church community.

Suicide Prevention Educational in the Black Church Questionnaire

Data Overview

This dataset includes responses about experiences, perceptions, and challenges faced by Black Church members regarding suicidal ideation and the availability of mental health support within their religious institutions. The qualitative responses highlight significant themes such as the reluctance to discuss suicidal thoughts with clergy, varying levels of awareness and presence of church-based mental health and counseling departments, and mixed feelings about the safety and comfort of addressing mental health issues within the church setting. By examining these responses, the data provide actionable recommendations to enhance the mental health support systems in Black Churches, promote open discussions, and foster a more supportive community environment for addressing mental health and suicide prevention. The respondents (n=24) ranged in age from 30 to 40 years, with a mean age of approximately 35 years. Fourteen (14) participants identified as female, seven (7) as male, and two (2) did not identify.

Qualitative and Quantitative Analysis

Common Themes

Wrestling with Suicidal Ideation and Embarrassment to Discuss with Clergy: Many respondents have not experienced suicidal ideation. Some have experienced suicidal ideation and felt embarrassed to discuss it with clergy.

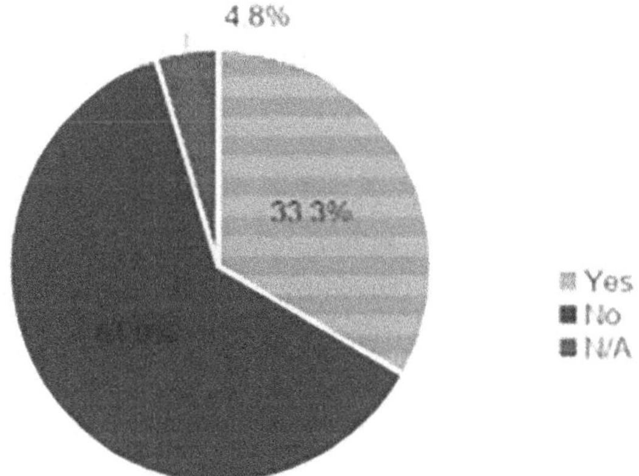

Figure 3. This pie graph illustrates responses to the question, "Have you in the past or present, wrestled with suicidal ideation that you were embarrassed to go to your pastor or other clergy in your church about? Why or why not?" (n=24).

Select Responses from Participants to Question in Figure 3:

> *"Yes, I have experienced suicidal ideation before I didn't go to my pastor or anybody about it because I felt as though it was something I could get over on my own."*
> *"Yes, because I was given the impression that you should "suck it up, you have God"."*
> *"I have never wrestled with suicidal ideations. But, if I did, I would feel comfortable only going to my pastor and no other minister in the church."*

"I actually went to one with intent to disclose yet my email was met with suggesting I was going about things wrong and how I should have honored them more by calling, so I didn't elaborate any deeper."

Church Mental Health and Counseling Department: The presence of mental health and counseling departments varies significantly across churches. Some respondents are unaware of such departments in their church (65.2% indicated that their church did not have a department and 13.0% was unsure).

Frequency of Addressing Suicide in Counseling Departments: Suicide is rarely addressed, even when counseling departments are present. Some churches rely on external health systems for mental health support. (Figure 4)

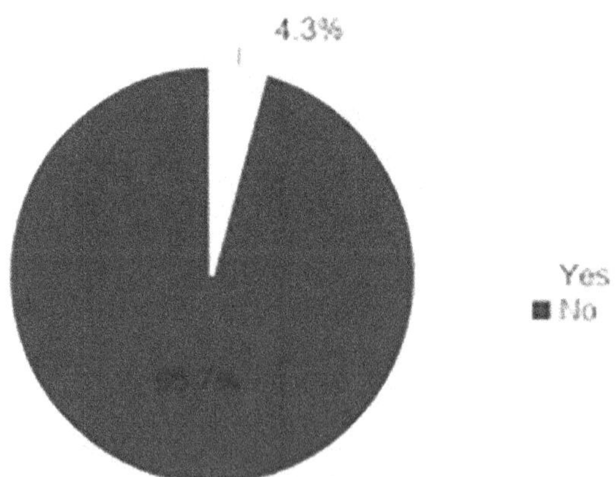

Figure 4. This pie graph illustrates responses to the question, "During Suicide Prevention Month (September), does your church hold workshops, bring in outside experts, or teach on Suicide awareness?" (n=24).

Comfort Level with Church Counseling Department for Suicidal Ideation: Comfort levels vary, with some respondents feeling comfortable and others not. Some respondents would only consider seeking help if their problems worsened.

Figure 4. This pie graph illustrates responses to the question, "If your church has a counseling department, would you feel comfortable going to them if you were experiencing thoughts of suicidal ideation?" (n=24).

Safety of Church as a Place to Discuss Mental Health: Mixed feelings about the church being a safe place for discussing mental health (21.7% did not believe that church is a safe place to discuss mental health, whereas 13.0% chose "N/A" and 66.2% responded "Yes"). Some respondents see the church as safe, while others do not or have conditional views.

Recommendations

Based on these key findings, churches should:

- Increase Awareness and Accessibility of Counseling Services.
- Regularly Address Mental Health Topics.
- Provide Training for Clergy and Church Leaders.

- Foster a Supportive Community Environment.
- Create a Safe and Confidential Space for Counseling.
- Collaborate with Mental Health Professionals.
- Clarify and Educate on Theological Views Regarding Mental Health.
- Provide Resources and Support Materials for Mental Health Education.

1. Increase Awareness and Accessibility of Counseling Services

- **Promote Existing Services:** Regularly inform church members about the availability of mental health counseling services, both locally and internationally.
- **Create Clear Communication Channels:** Ensure that church members know how to access these services confidentially.

2. Regularly Address Mental Health Topics

- **Incorporate Mental Health in Sermons and Teachings:** Include discussions on mental health and suicide prevention in sermons, Bible studies, and other teaching sessions.
- **Host Workshops and Seminars:** Organize regular workshops with mental health professionals to provide education and training to both clergy and congregants.

3. Training for Clergy and Church Leaders

- **Provide Mental Health First Aid Training:** Equip clergy and church leaders with basic training on recognizing and responding to mental health issues.
- **Develop a Referral System:** Train leaders on how to refer individuals to appropriate mental health professionals and resources.

4. Foster a Supportive Community Environment

- **Encourage Open Discussions:** Create a church culture where discussing mental health issues is normalized and encouraged.
- **Support Groups:** Establish support groups within the church for individuals struggling with mental health issues or affected by suicide.

5. Create a Safe and Confidential Space

- **Confidential Counseling:** Ensure that counseling services are confidential, and members feel safe to share their struggles without fear of judgment.
- **Anonymous Feedback:** Allow members to provide anonymous feedback on their experiences and suggestions for improving mental health support within the church.

6. Collaborate with Mental Health Professionals

- **Partnerships:** Partner with local mental health organizations and professionals to provide expert support and resources.
- **Guest Speakers:** Invite mental health professionals to speak at church events and services.

7. Address Theological Views on Mental Health

- **Clarify Church's Stance:** Clearly communicate the church's theological views on mental health and suicide, emphasizing compassion and support.
- **Theological Education:** Educate the congregation on how faith and mental health can coexist, addressing any misconceptions that may prevent people from seeking help.

8. Provide Resources and Support Materials

- **Educational Materials:** Distribute pamphlets, books, and other resources that provide information on mental health and suicide prevention.
- **Online Resources:** Utilize the church's website and social media to share mental health resources and information.

By implementing these recommendations, churches can better support their members' mental health needs and create a more open and supportive environment for discussing and addressing critical issues related to mental health and suicide prevention.

Suicide Survey for the Black Church Members

Data Overview

This analysis is of the survey data collected from members of Black church communities regarding their views on mental health and suicide awareness and prevention. The data includes both quantitative and qualitative responses, predominately Likert scale, providing a comprehensive understanding of the current state of mental health support within these communities. The analysis aims to identify key patterns, satisfaction levels, perceptions, and suggestions for improvement. The survey received responses from 28 participants. The respondents' ages ranged from 29 to 39 years, with an average age of approximately 34 years. Ten (10) participants identified as male, fourteen (14) as female, and three (3) did not identify.

Quantitative Analysis

The frequency of responses for each survey question highlights the general sentiments and levels of satisfaction among the participants:

- **Satisfaction with Church's Strategic Planning on Suicide Awareness and Prevention**: Figure 5 shows the distribution of responses, with a notable proportion expressing disappointment (63.0%).

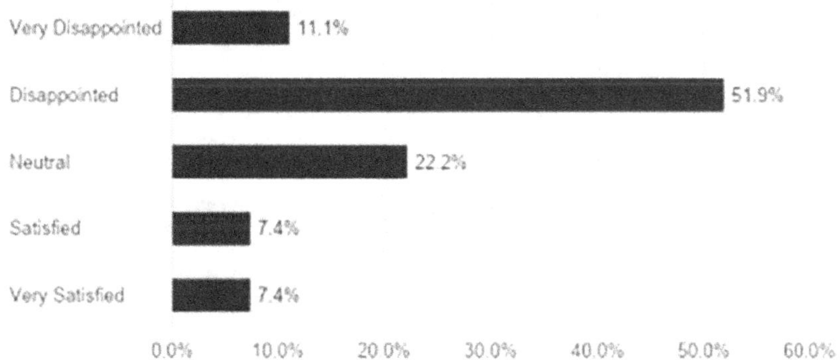

Figure 5. This graph illustrates responses to the question, "I am satisfied with my church's strategic planning on suicide awareness and prevention" (n=28).

- **Perception of Church's Seriousness about Mental Health**: Figure 6 illustrates varied responses, with a significant number of respondents feeling satisfied or very satisfied, while others are neutral or disappointed.

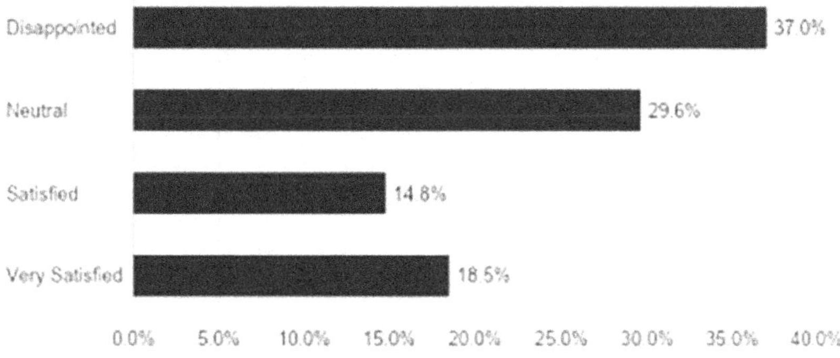

Figure 6. This graph illustrates responses to the question, "I feel that my church takes mental health very seriously" (n=28).

- **Trust in Clergy's Confidentiality Regarding Mental Health**: Figure 7 illustrates that many respondents feel very satisfied or satisfied, indicating a high level of trust in clergy confidentiality.

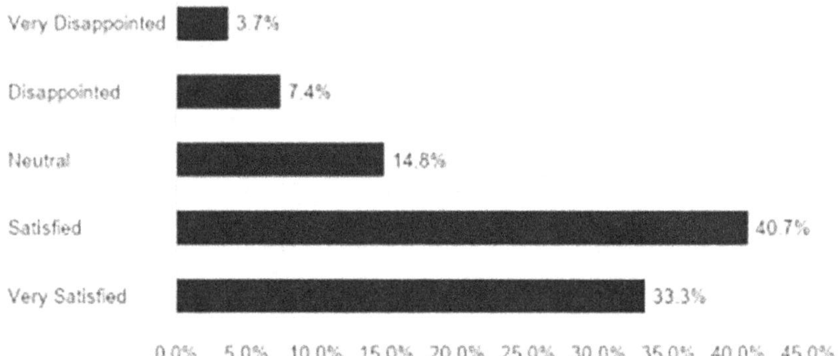

Figure 7. This graph illustrates responses to the question, "I can trust in the confidentiality of the clergy at my church regarding my mental health, with the exception of suicide ideations, knowing it's an Ethical matter to report." (n=28).

- **Church's Approach to the Topic of Suicide**: The responses in Figure 8 indicate mixed feelings, with some members very satisfied, while others are neutral or very disappointed.

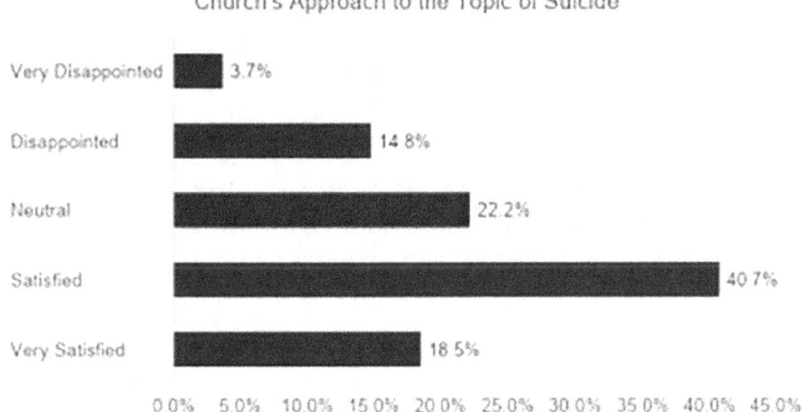

Figure 8. This graph illustrates responses to the question, "I feel that the church deals with the topic of suicide from a place of love without negating Biblical truths on the subject matter." (n=28).

- **Perception of Whether Church Considers Members' Input on Suicide Awareness and Prevention**: Figure 9 highlights that while many feel very satisfied, there are also neutral and disappointed responses, suggesting room for improvement.

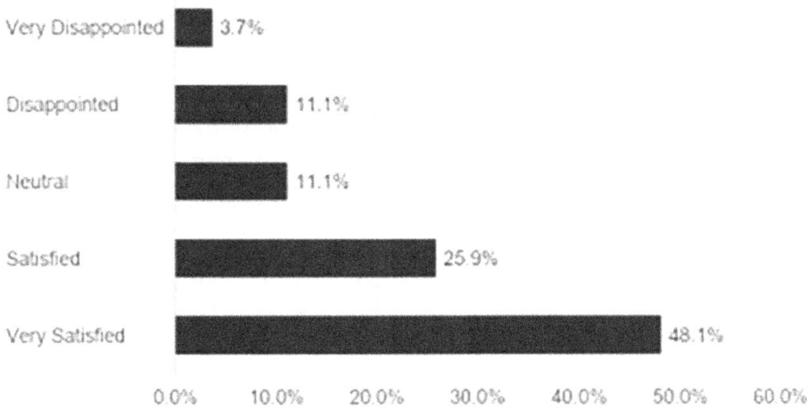

Figure 9. This graph illustrates responses to the question, "My input on what the church could incorporate on suicide awareness and prevention will be considered." (n=28).

Qualitative Analysis

The survey results reveal mixed feelings among church members regarding the current state of mental health and suicide awareness initiatives. While there is a high level of trust in clergy confidentiality, many respondents are dissatisfied with the church's strategic planning and approach to mental health. The thematic analysis identified the following common themes:

Theme	Frequency Common Suggestions
Increased Education and Awareness	HighRegular workshops, seminars, informational sessions about mental health and suicide prevention
Support Groups and Counseling	HighEstablishment of support groups, accessible counseling services for ongoing mental health support
Confidentiality and Trust	Moderate Measures to ensure privacy of discussions, building trust with church leaders
Integration of Faith and Mental Health	ModerateBalanced approach combining biblical teachings with modern mental health practices
Training for Clergy and Church Leaders	Moderate More training for clergy and church leaders on mental health issues and suicide prevention

- **Increased Education and Awareness Programs**: Many respondents emphasized the need for regular workshops, seminars, and informational sessions to educate church members about mental health and suicide prevention.
- **Support Groups and Counseling Services**: There was a strong call for the establishment of support groups

and accessible counseling services to provide ongoing mental health support.

- **Confidentiality and Trust**: Ensuring confidentiality and building trust were highlighted as crucial for creating a safe environment for discussing mental health issues without fear of judgment.
- **Integration of Faith and Mental Health**: Respondents advocated for a balanced approach that integrates biblical teachings with modern mental health practices to promote a holistic understanding of mental well-being.
- **Training for Clergy and Church Leaders**: Many participants recommended more training for clergy and church leaders to equip them with the knowledge and skills needed to address mental health issues and provide effective suicide prevention support.

The survey results indicate that while there is trust in clergy confidentiality, there is a clear need for improved strategic planning and awareness programs regarding mental health and suicide prevention within the church. Respondents advocate for increased education, support services, integration of faith and mental health practices, and better training for church leaders. Addressing these areas can help create a more supportive and informed church environment for members dealing with mental health issues.

Qualitative Interviews of Black Licensed Professionals

Data Overview

This is an in-depth analysis of responses from qualitative interviews conducted with Black licensed mental health professionals. The interviews explore their motivations, personal experiences with mental health, perspectives on the church's role in mental health education, and strategies for clergy to address suicidality. The thematic analysis reveals commonalities that provide insights into the intersection of personal, community, and spiritual influences on their professional journeys.

Quantitative Analysis

The following analysis lists common themes explored by each response to the associated question:

- ***QUESTION 1**: As a congregant in the Black church and African American, what drove you to be a licensed mental health professional?*

The responses share several **common themes**:

Unexpected Career Path Many respondents did not initially plan to become mental health professionals. Their career journeys started with different intentions, such as becoming an elementary school teacher or a nurse. This indicates a common theme of career paths that evolved over time due to various influences.

Personal Influence and Experiences Personal and familial experiences significantly influenced the decision to pursue mental health professions. These include direct experiences with mental health issues within their families, personal struggles, and a sense of divine or spiritual guidance.

Passion for Helping Others A strong desire to help others, particularly within their own communities, emerged as a key motivator. Respondents expressed a calling to address the specific needs and challenges faced by the African American community, such as high divorce rates and lack of mental health support.

Awareness of Community Needs There is a heightened awareness among respondents about the mental health challenges within the Black community. This awareness, combined with personal and spiritual motivations, drives their commitment to the profession.

- ***QUESTION 2:*** *Have you struggles with Mental Health/ Suicide yourself?*

The responses to the question about struggling with mental health or suicide share several **common themes**:

Personal Experience with Mental Health Issues All respondents shared personal experiences with mental health challenges, including severe thoughts of suicide, depression, anxiety, and complex grief. This personal connection to mental health struggles adds depth to their professional empathy and understanding.

Lack of Support from Traditional Sources A recurring theme is the inadequate support from traditional sources such as family and the church. Respondents often felt demonized or misunderstood by their religious communities and family members when they sought help for mental health issues.

Church and Spiritual Conflicts Several respondents highlighted conflicts between their mental health struggles and the teachings or responses from their religious communities. Misconceptions about mental health, such as viewing depression as a spiritual failing, were common.

Evolution of Understanding There is a notable evolution in the respondents' understanding of mental health. Initially, many experienced stigma and confusion but eventually developed a clearer understanding of the importance of therapy and professional support.

Cultural Stigma The broader cultural stigma surrounding mental health within the Black community and the Black church is evident. This stigma often prevents open discussion and seeking help for mental health issues.

- ***QUESTION 3***: *How Important is the Topic of Suicide and should the church be educated on it?*

Recognition of the Importance All respondents emphasized the critical need to address suicide and mental health issues within the church. They agreed that these topics are essential and require urgent attention.

Need for Non-Judgmental Support Creating a supportive and non-judgmental environment within the church is vital. Respondents called for spaces where individuals can discuss their mental health struggles without fear of judgment.

Misconceptions and Stigma Misconceptions within the church, particularly attributing mental health issues to demonic attacks or spiritual failings, are problematic. Such stigmatization prevents individuals from seeking appropriate help.

Educational Need There is a strong need for education on mental health and suicide within the church. Respondents emphasized the importance of understanding both the natural and spiritual aspects of mental health.

Role of Church Leadership Church leaders play a significant role in addressing mental health. Educating clergy and integrating mental health understanding into church leadership is crucial for making a positive impact.

Integration of Mental Health Support Some respondents suggested integrating mental health support within church activities. This involves creating mental health teams and combining spiritual care with mental health support.

- ***QUESTION 4**: How should clergy who aren't educated confront this topic and be equipped to assist parishioners who struggle with suicidal ideations?*

Referral to Professionals Clergy should refer individuals to mental health professionals and community care centers. Recognizing the limits of their expertise, clergy are encouraged to connect parishioners with appropriate professional help.

Education and Training Clergy need education and training to handle mental health crises, understand appropriate protocols, and know when to involve authorities or mental health experts.

Understanding Limitations Effective pastoral care involves acknowledging limitations and recognizing when professional intervention is necessary. Clergy should avoid the pretense of having all the answers.

Practical Steps and Protocols Clergy should understand and follow specific protocols to ensure the safety and well-being of individuals expressing suicidal ideations. Knowing when to call 911 or a psychiatrist is crucial.

Addressing Historical and Cultural Contexts Understanding the historical and cultural contexts of mental health within the Black community and the Black church is important. This includes recognizing past practices of hiding mental health struggles and advocating for accountability and awareness.

Combining Prayer with Action While prayer is valuable, it should be combined with actionable steps to ensure individuals receive necessary mental health support.

- ***QUESTION 5***: *How important is it for the church to understand the link between trauma and suicidality?*

Necessity of Education and Workshops The church should engage in continuous educational efforts, such as workshops, to understand the connection between trauma and suicidality.

Combating Misconceptions Moving away from misconceptions about mental health issues, such as attributing them solely to demonic influences, is necessary. A balanced approach that includes both faith and professional support is advocated.

Holistic Understanding of Trauma Understanding the deep and pervasive impact of trauma on individuals is crucial. This includes recognizing its effects on the body, mind, and core beliefs.

Integration of Heart and Mind Addressing both spiritual and emotional needs is essential for true healing. Respondents suggest that healing involves acknowledging and addressing emotional fractures, not just focusing on spiritual formation.

Professional and Spiritual Collaboration A collaborative approach involving both professional mental health care and spiritual support is necessary. This recognizes the limits of pastoral care and the importance of specialized mental health expertise.

Recognition of Statistics and Reality Understanding statistics related to trauma and suicide is important. The church should be informed by data and real-world evidence to grasp the urgency and scale of the issue.

Holistic Healing Aiming for holistic healing, the church should strive to address the whole person—spiritually, emotionally, and mentally—rather than focusing on one aspect alone.

The analysis of qualitative interviews with Black licensed professionals reveals a complex interplay of personal, spiritual, and community-driven motivations and experiences. These professionals navigate cultural stigmas, misconceptions, and the need for education within the Black church to address mental health and suicidality effectively. The insights gained highlight the importance of holistic, collaborative approaches that integrate professional mental health support with spiritual care.

Afterword

Just Keep Talking

The Black Church must find the courage to keep the conversation alive regarding this critical issue. Ministering to those who are suicidal is ministry—it's Kingdom ministry. King Jesus came so that we could have life, and life more abundantly. While there is still much work to be done, the conversation must begin today. It must take place in our pulpits on Sunday mornings and in our Bible studies throughout the week, whether in person or on Zoom. The conversation must also occur in our workshops and conferences.

This needs to be a collaborative discussion between the Black Church and mental health professionals, including psychologists, psychiatrists, licensed clinical mental health therapists, and hospitals. Consultation is crucial when it comes to suicide prevention. We must remember that great things begin with a conversation. Suicide prevention begins with a conversation. Most importantly, when we are educated on crisis and suicide prevention, we will know how to respond to those struggling with suicide within the walls of the Black Church.

Appendix

ANALYSIS – Responses to Qualitative Interviews of Black Licensed Professionals

→ QUESTION 1: *As a congregant in the Black church and African American, what drove you to be a licensed mental health professional?*

The responses share several **common themes**:

1. **Unexpected Career Path**: Each respondent mentions an initial career intention or influence that was different from becoming a mental health professional (e.g., elementary school teacher, nurse, nursing major). Their paths to mental health professions were not originally planned.

2. **Personal Influence and Experiences**: Personal experiences and influences played a significant role in their career choices. This includes family influences, personal or family mental health experiences, and divine or spiritual guidance.

3. **Passion for Helping Others**: Each response indicates a strong desire or passion to help others, particularly within their communities. This drive seems to stem from a combination of personal experience, a calling, and a recognition of the needs within the African American community.

4. **Awareness of Community Needs**: There is an awareness of specific mental health challenges and needs within the Black community. For example, one response

mentions high divorce rates and another highlights the lack of mental health support for Black families.

These shared elements reflect a blend of personal, spiritual, and community-driven motivations for becoming licensed mental health professionals.

→ QUESTION 2: *Have you struggles with Mental Health/Suicide yourself?*

The responses to the question about struggling with mental health or suicide share several **common themes**:

1. **Personal Experience with Mental Health Issues**: Each respondent has experienced mental health challenges, whether it be severe thoughts of suicide, depression, anxiety, or complex grief. This indicates a personal connection to mental health struggles.
2. **Lack of Support from Traditional Sources**: There is a recurring theme of inadequate support from traditional sources such as family and the church. Respondents mention feeling demonized, misunderstood, or not supported by their church or family when dealing with mental health issues.
3. **Church and Spiritual Conflicts**: Several respondents highlight conflicts between their mental health struggles and the teachings or responses from their religious communities. Issues such as being told that depression and anxiety were spirits, or not finding help within the church, are mentioned.
4. **Evolution of Understanding**: There is an element of growth in understanding mental health. Respondents have moved from initial confusion or stigma (e.g., thinking they were possessed) to a clearer understanding of mental health issues and the importance of therapy and proper support.

5. **Cultural Stigma**: The responses reflect the broader cultural stigma surrounding mental health within the Black community and the Black church, including the reluctance to talk about these issues openly and seek help.

Overall, these commonalities reflect the personal and cultural challenges faced in addressing mental health issues within the context of the Black community and the Black church.

→ QUESTION *3: How Important is the Topic of Suicide and should the church be educated on it?*

The responses to the question about the importance of the topic of suicide and whether the church should be educated on it share several **common themes**:

1. **Recognition of the Importance:** Each respondent emphasizes the critical importance of addressing the topic of suicide and mental health within the church. They unanimously agree that this is an essential issue that needs attention.
2. **Need for Non-Judgmental Support**: There is a call for creating a supportive and non-judgmental environment within the church. Respondents recognize the need for the church to provide a space where individuals can discuss their mental health struggles without fear of judgment.
3. **Misconceptions and Stigma**: Several responses highlight the problem of misconceptions within the church, particularly the tendency to attribute mental health issues to demonic attacks or spiritual failings. This stigmatization can prevent individuals from seeking appropriate help.
4. **Educational Need**: The responses indicate a strong need for education on mental health and suicide within

the church. This includes understanding the natural and spiritual aspects of mental health and recognizing that prayer alone may not be sufficient to address these issues.

5. **Role of Church Leadership**: There is an acknowledgment of the significant role church leaders play in addressing mental health. Educating clergy and integrating mental health understanding into church leadership is seen as crucial for making a positive impact.

6. **Integration of Mental Health Support**: Some responses suggest the integration of mental health support within church activities, emphasizing collaboration rather than segmentation. This approach involves creating mental health teams and combining spiritual and mental health care.

Overall, these commonalities reflect a shared recognition of the importance of addressing mental health and suicide in the church, the need to overcome stigma and misconceptions, and the importance of education and support systems to effectively help congregants.

→ QUESTION 4: *How should clergy who aren't educated confront this topic and be equipped to assist parishioners who struggle with suicidal ideations?*

The responses to the question about how clergy who aren't educated should confront the topic of suicide and be equipped to assist parishioners who struggle with suicidal ideations share several **common themes**:

1. **Referral to Professionals**: Each response emphasizes the importance of clergy referring individuals to mental health professionals and community care centers. Recognizing the limits of their expertise, clergy are

encouraged to connect parishioners with appropriate professional help.

2. **Education and Training**: There is a clear call for clergy to become educated and trained in handling mental health crises, including understanding the appropriate protocols and knowing when to call authorities or mental health experts.

3. **Understanding Limitations**: The responses highlight the need for clergy to acknowledge their limitations and avoid the pretense of having all the answers. Effective pastoral care involves recognizing when professional intervention is necessary.

4. **Practical Steps and Protocols**: Practical steps, such as knowing when to call 911 or a psychiatrist, are emphasized. Clergy are encouraged to understand and follow specific protocols to ensure the safety and well-being of individuals expressing suicidal ideations.

5. **Addressing Historical and Cultural Contexts**: One response points out the importance of understanding the historical and cultural contexts of mental health within the Black community and the Black church. This includes recognizing past practices of hiding mental health struggles and advocating for accountability and awareness in addressing mental health today.

6. **Combining Prayer with Action**: While prayer is acknowledged as valuable, it is not seen as a standalone solution. Clergy are urged to combine prayer with actionable steps that ensure individuals receive the necessary mental health support.

Overall, these commonalities reflect a holistic approach to addressing mental health and suicidal ideations within the church, combining spiritual care with professional mental health support, education, practical protocols, and an understanding of cultural history.

→ QUESTION 5: *How important is it for the church to understand the link between trauma and suicidality?*

The responses to the question about the importance of the church understanding the link between trauma and suicidality share several **common themes**:

1. **Necessity of Education and Workshops**: Each response emphasizes the need for the church to engage in educational efforts, such as workshops, to better understand the connection between trauma and suicidality. Continuous learning is highlighted as a critical component.

2. **Combating Misconceptions**: There is a call to move away from misconceptions, such as attributing mental health issues solely to demonic influences. The responses advocate for a balanced approach that includes both faith and professional mental health support.

3. **Holistic Understanding of Trauma**: Respondents stress the importance of understanding trauma's deep and pervasive impact on individuals, including its effects on the body, mind, and core beliefs. This holistic understanding is crucial for effective support and intervention.

4. **Integration of Heart and Mind**: The importance of addressing both spiritual and emotional needs is highlighted. The responses suggest that true healing involves acknowledging and healing the fractures in the heart, not just focusing on spiritual formation.

5. **Professional and Spiritual Collaboration**: The responses emphasize the need for a collaborative approach that involves both professional mental health care and spiritual support. This recognizes the limits of pastoral care and the importance of specialized mental health expertise.

6. **Recognition of Statistics and Reality**: One response points to the importance of understanding statistics related to trauma and suicide, indicating a need for the church to be informed by data and real-world evidence to grasp the urgency and scale of the issue.
7. **Holistic Healing**: The goal of holistic healing is a common thread, suggesting that the church should strive to address the whole person—spiritually, emotionally, and mentally—rather than focusing on one aspect alone.

Overall, these commonalities reflect a comprehensive approach that includes education, addressing misconceptions, understanding trauma's impact, integrating emotional and spiritual care, collaborating with mental health professionals, and aiming for holistic healing.

ANALYSIS - SUICIDE EDUCATION
AMONG CLERGY QUESTIONNAIRE

OBSERVATIONS FROM QUANTITATIVE ANALYSIS:

Frequency of Psycho-education:

Respondents vary in how often they engage in psycho-education about suicide, with some engaging often while others rarely do so.

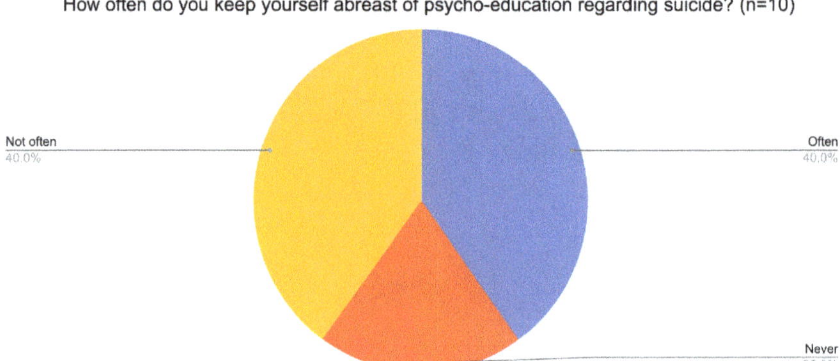

Certification in Suicide Prevention:

A significant portion of respondents are not certified in suicide prevention, although many have taken related courses.

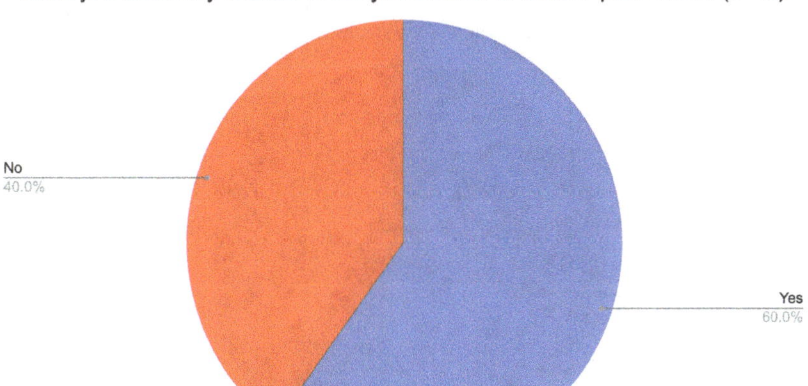

Importance of Suicide Topic:

The topic of suicide is highly important to most respondents, with many rating it 10 out of 10 (8 out of 10 rated 10, the other two were 6 and 8). 100% of respondents believe in Christian Psychology.

Addressing Suicide Issue:

Most respondents have been asked to address suicide issues from the pulpit and other platforms.

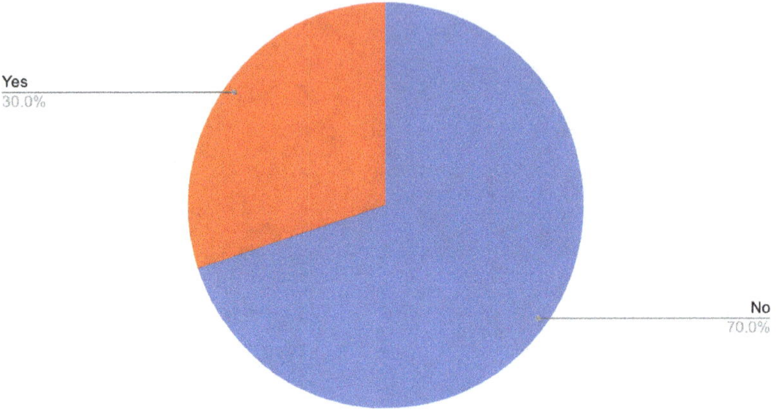

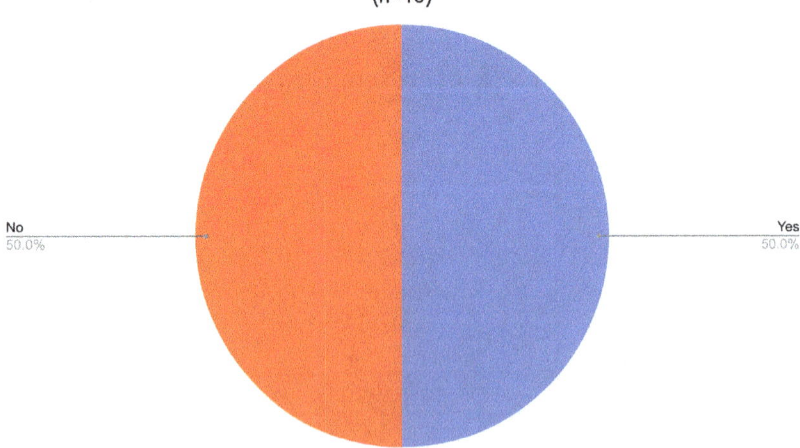

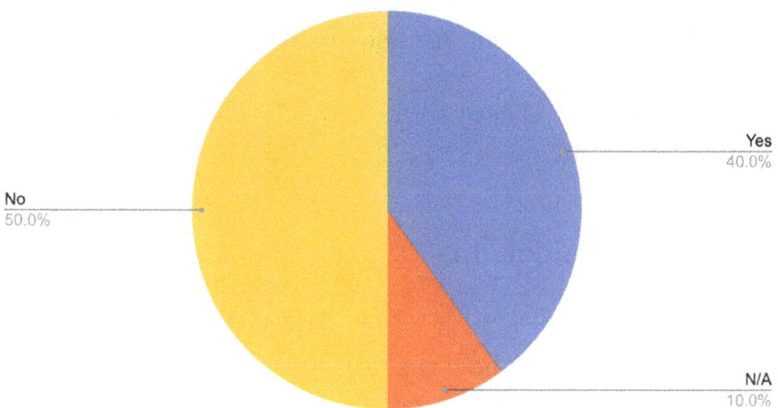

Personal Suicidal Ideations:

A notable number of respondents have struggled with suicidal ideations themselves.

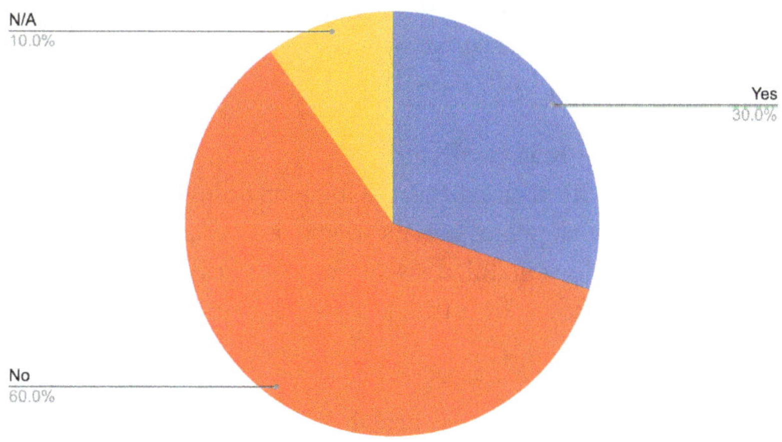

Demographics:

Age Distribution: Respondents span a wide range of ages, with a noticeable number in their 30s and 50s.

Gender Distribution: There were 7 out of 10 respondents who identified as "male".

Key Recommendations

From the qualitative responses, several key themes and recommendations emerge on how the church can better serve congregants who struggle with mental health:

1. **Raising Awareness:**
   - Establish mental health or counseling ministries.
   - Increase awareness of mental health topics within the church.

2. **Open Dialogue:**
   - Create spaces for open discussions about mental health and suicide.
   - Normalize conversations about mental health similar to physical health.

3. **Professional Involvement:**
   - Invite trained therapists, psychologists, and mental health professionals to speak to congregations.
   - Hold scheduled sessions and workshops focused on suicide prevention and mental health.

4. **Reducing Stigma:**
   - Address mental health issues without condemning or trivializing them.
   - Approach mental health with compassion and understanding, avoiding judgmental attitudes.

5. **Education:**
   - Educate congregants about mental health and the relationship between mental health conditions and suicide.
   - Decrease stigma and erroneous interpretations of scripture related to mental health and suicidality.

6. **Support Systems:**
   - Establish support systems within the church to assist those in need.
   - Create a safe and non-judgmental environment where people can openly discuss their struggles.

7. **Advocacy:**
   - Engage in advocacy at the local level to support mental health initiatives.
   - Promote mental health awareness and suicide prevention actively within the community.

8. **Trauma-Informed Approach:**
   - Become trauma-informed and friendly towards psychiatric care.
   - Recognize and address the impact of trauma on mental health.

Conclusion

The recommendations emphasize the need for churches to be proactive in addressing mental health issues, fostering open dialogue, reducing stigma, involving professionals, and providing comprehensive support to congregants. These steps can significantly contribute to better mental health outcomes within the church community.

ANALYSIS – Suicide Prevention Education in the Black Church Member Questionnaire

Summary of Qualitative Responses:

1. Wrestling with Suicidal Ideation and Embarrassment to Discuss with Clergy:
   - Responses: "No," "Yes," and some missing (NA).
   - Common Themes:
     - Many respondents have not experienced suicidal ideation.
     - Some respondents have experienced suicidal ideation and felt embarrassed to discuss it with clergy.

2. Church Mental Health and Counseling Department:
   - Responses: "Yes," "No," "On the international level," "I don't know," and some missing (nan).
   - Common Themes:
     - Presence of mental health and counseling departments varies significantly across churches.
     - Some respondents are unaware of such departments in their church.

3. Frequency of Addressing Suicide in Counseling Departments:
   - Responses: "Yes, however, suicide is rarely addressed," "No local counseling department, but the local health system helps," "No," "Yes counseling and counselors are available," and some missing (nan).
   - Common Themes:
     - Suicide is rarely addressed, even when counseling departments are present.

- Some churches rely on external health systems for mental health support.

4. Comfort Level with Church Counseling Department for Suicidal Ideation:
   - Responses: "Yes," "No," "If and only if my problems get worse," and some missing (nan).
   - Common Themes:
     - Comfort levels vary, with some respondents feeling comfortable and others not.
     - Some respondents would only consider seeking help if their problems worsened.

5. Safety of Church as a Place to Discuss Mental Health:
   - Responses: "Yes," "No," "Yes and no," and some missing (nan).
   - Common Themes:
     - Mixed feelings about the church being a safe place for discussing mental health.
     - Some respondents see the church as safe, while others do not or have conditional views.

Key Findings from the Analysis

1. **Age and Gender Distribution:**
   - The majority of respondents are in the 30-40 age range.
   - There is a higher representation of female respondents compared to males.

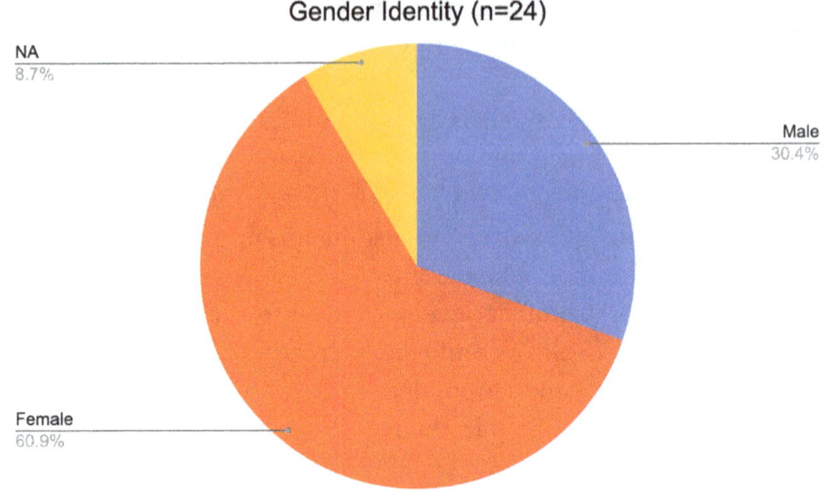

2. **Mental Health and Suicidal Ideation:**
   - A significant number of respondents have not experienced suicidal ideation.
   - Some respondents have experienced suicidal ideation and felt embarrassed to discuss it with clergy.

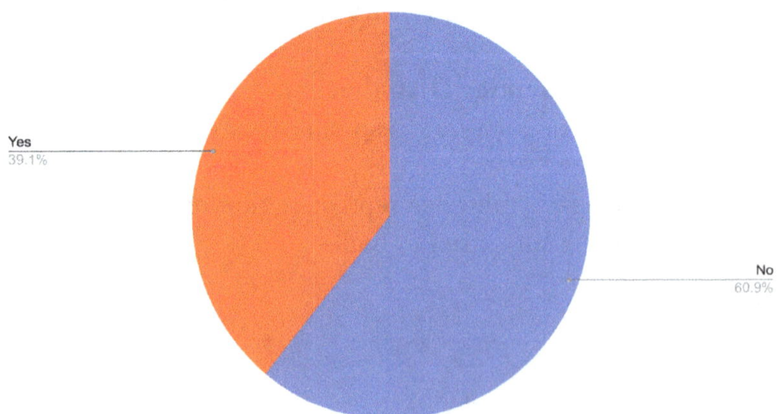

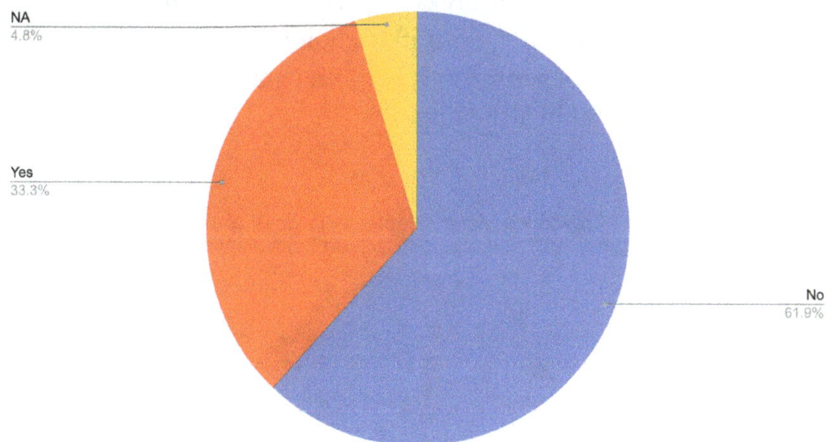

3. **Availability and Awareness of Counseling Departments:**
   - Mixed availability of mental health and counseling departments within churches.
   - Some respondents are unaware of the existence of such departments in their church.

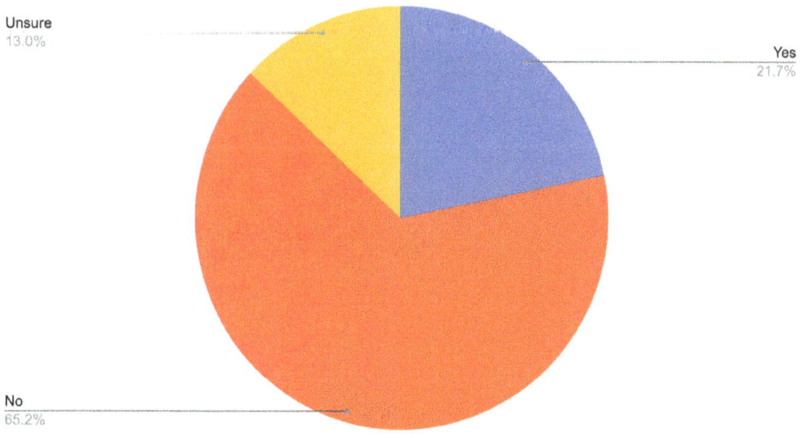

4. **Addressing Suicide in Counseling Departments:**
   - Suicide is rarely addressed in church counseling departments, even if such departments exist.
   - Churches often rely on external health systems for mental health support.

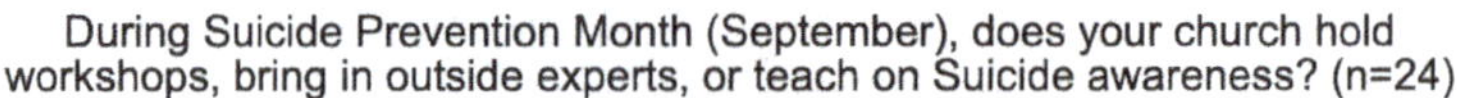

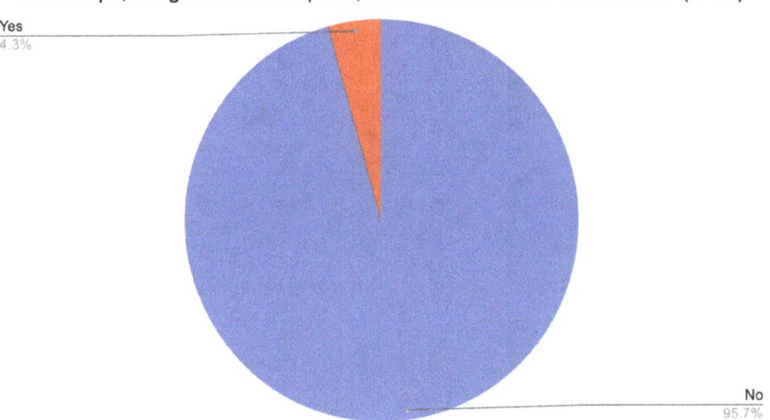

5. **Comfort Level with Church Counseling Services:**
   - Comfort levels with seeking help from church counseling departments vary among respondents.
   - Some respondents are comfortable seeking help, while others would only do so if their problems worsened.

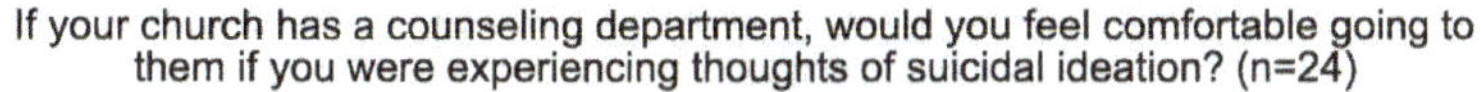

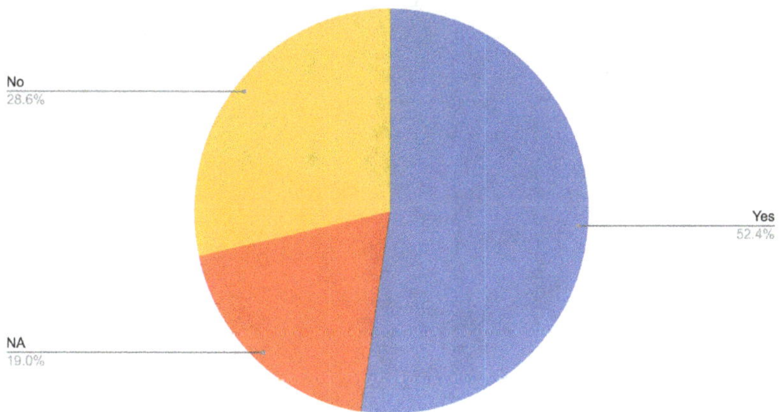

6. **Perception of Church as a Safe Place for Mental Health Discussions:**
   - Mixed feelings about whether the church is a safe place to discuss mental health.
   - Some respondents see the church as a safe place, while others do not or have conditional views.

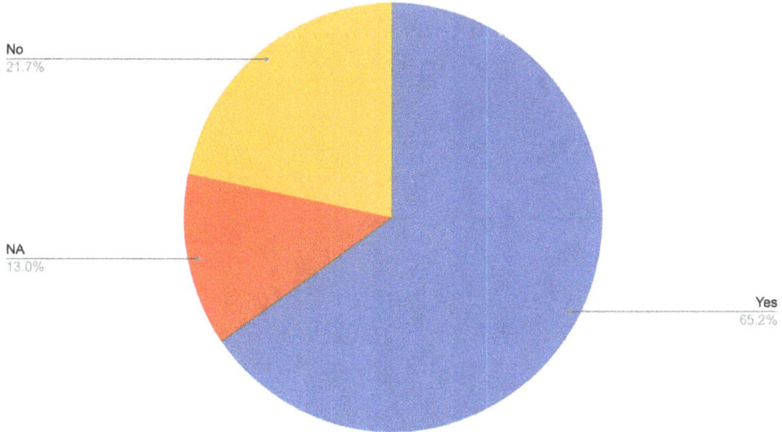

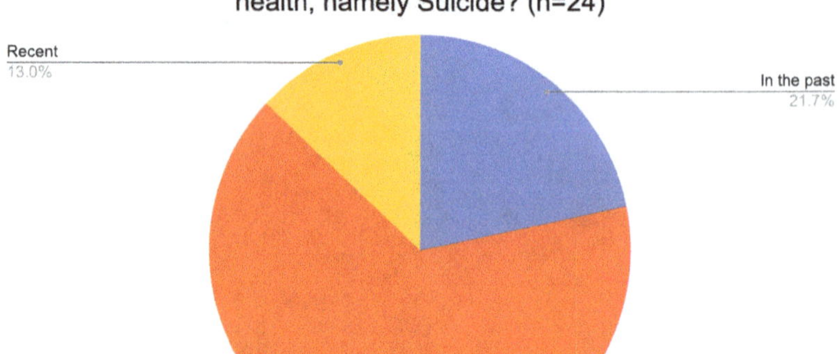

General Recommendations

Based on these key findings, churches should:

- Increase Awareness and Accessibility of Counseling Services.
- Regularly Address Mental Health Topics.
- Provide Training for Clergy and Church Leaders.
- Foster a Supportive Community Environment.
- Create a Safe and Confidential Space for Counseling.
- Collaborate with Mental Health Professionals.
- Clarify and Educate on Theological Views Regarding Mental Health.
- Provide Resources and Support Materials for Mental Health Education.

These actions can help churches better support their members' mental health needs and create a more open and supportive environment for discussing and addressing these critical issues.

Recommended Actions for Churches

1. **Increase Awareness and Accessibility of Counseling Services:**
   - Promote Existing Services: Regularly inform church members about the availability of mental health counseling services, both at the local and international levels.
   - Create Clear Communication Channels: Ensure that church members know how to access these services confidentially.

2. **Regularly Address Mental Health Topics:**
   - Incorporate Mental Health in Sermons and Teachings: Include discussions on mental health and suicide prevention in sermons, Bible studies, and other teaching sessions.
   - Host Workshops and Seminars: Organize regular workshops, bringing in mental health professionals to provide education and training to both clergy and congregants.

3. **Training for Clergy and Church Leaders:**
   - Provide Mental Health First Aid Training: Equip clergy and church leaders with basic training on how to recognize and respond to mental health issues.
   - Develop a Referral System: Train leaders on how to refer individuals to appropriate mental health professionals and resources.

4. **Foster a Supportive Community Environment:**
   - Encourage Open Discussions: Create a church culture where discussing mental health issues is normalized and encouraged.
   - Support Groups: Establish support groups within the church for individuals struggling with mental health issues or who have been affected by suicide.

5. **Create a Safe and Confidential Space:**
   - Confidential Counseling: Ensure that the counseling services provided are confidential and that members feel safe to share their struggles without fear of judgment.
   - Anonymous Feedback: Allow members to provide anonymous feedback on their experiences and suggestions for improving mental health support within the church.

6. **Collaborate with Mental Health Professionals:**
   - Partnerships: Partner with local mental health organizations and professionals to provide expert support and resources.
   - Guest Speakers: Invite mental health professionals to speak at church events and services.

7. **Address Theological Views on Mental Health:**
   - Clarify Church's Stance: Clearly communicate the church's theological views on mental health and suicide, emphasizing compassion and support.
   - Theological Education: Educate the congregation on how faith and mental health can coexist, addressing any misconceptions that may prevent people from seeking help.

8. **Provide Resources and Support Materials:**
   - Educational Materials: Distribute pamphlets, books, and other resources that provide information on mental health and suicide prevention.
   - Online Resources: Utilize the church's website and social media to share mental health resources and information.

By taking these actions, churches can become a more supportive and proactive environment for addressing mental health issues and preventing suicide within their communities.

225

ANALYSIS - SUICIDE SURVEY FOR THE BLACK CHURCH MEMBERS

Quantitative Data Analysis (n=28)

Satisfaction with Church's Strategic Planning on Suicide Awareness and Prevention

- The graph shows the distribution of responses, with a notable proportion expressing disappointment.

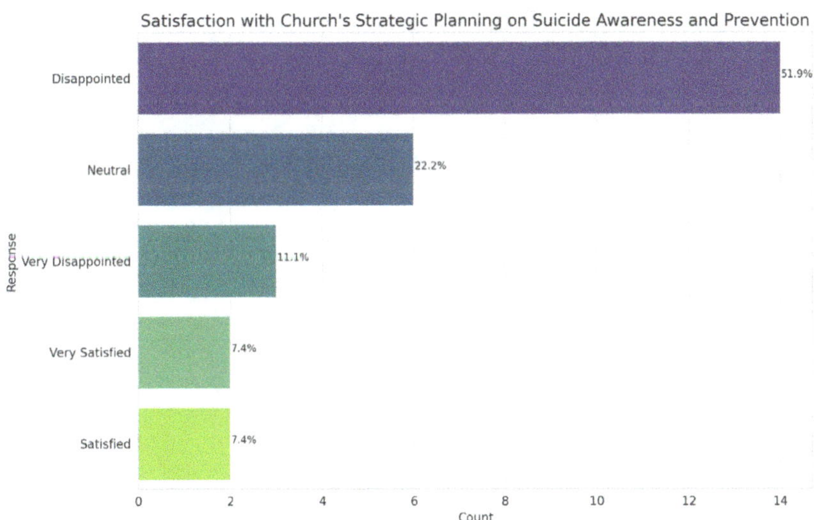

Perception of Church's Seriousness about Mental Health

The responses are varied, with a significant number of respondents feeling satisfied or very satisfied, while others are neutral or disappointed.

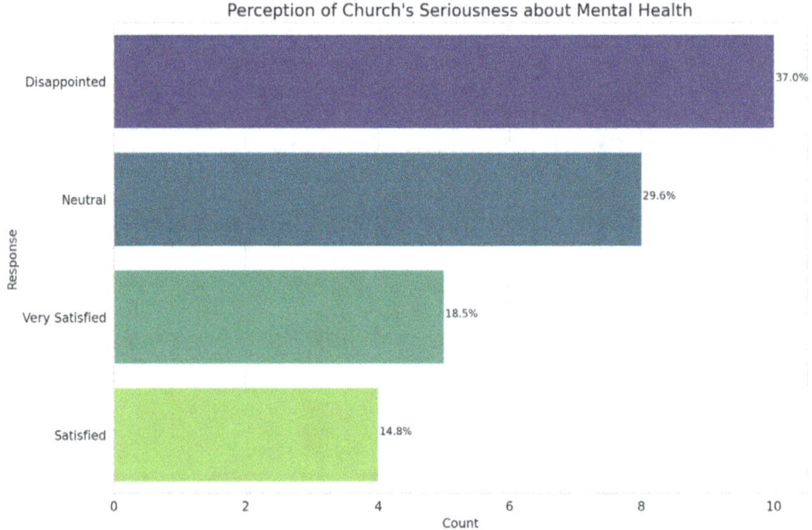

Trust in Clergy's Confidentiality Regarding Mental Health

Many respondents feel very satisfied or satisfied, indicating a high level of trust in clergy confidentiality.

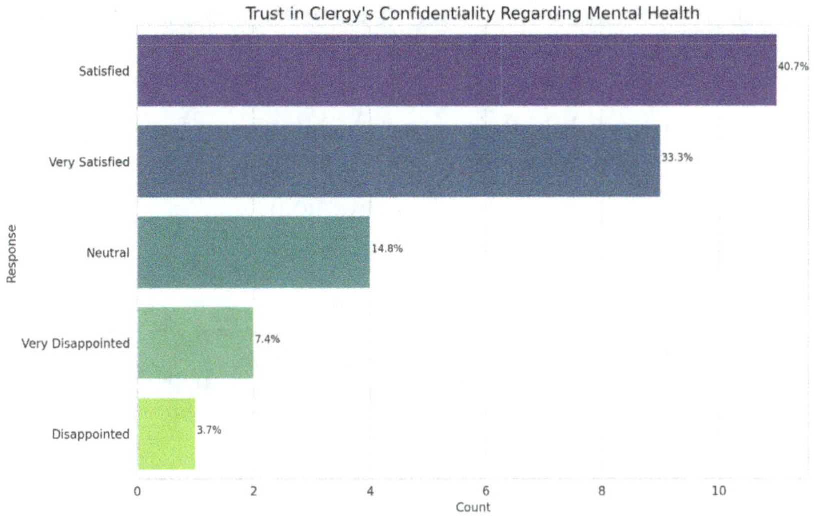

Church's Approach to the Topic of Suicide

- The responses indicate mixed feelings, with some members very satisfied, while others are neutral or very disappointed.

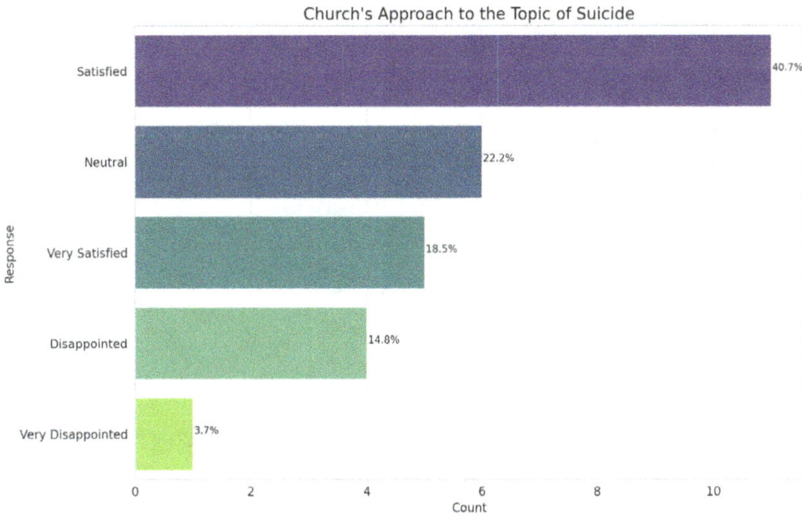

Perception of Whether Church Considers Members' Input on Suicide Awareness and Prevention

- The graph highlights that while many feel very satisfied, there are also neutral and disappointed responses, suggesting room for improvement.

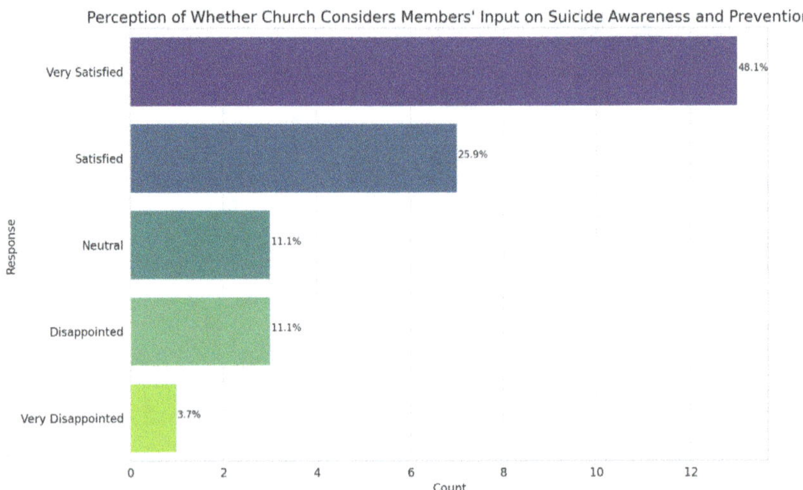

Qualitative Data Analysis

The survey includes qualitative feedback on what the church could incorporate regarding suicide awareness and prevention. Common themes among these responses will be identified by examining recurring ideas and suggestions.

Themes:

1. **Increased Education and Awareness Programs**: Many respondents suggested implementing more education and awareness programs within the church to address mental health and suicide.

2. **Support Groups and Counseling Services**: Several responses emphasized the need for support groups and counseling services to provide ongoing support to members struggling with mental health issues.

3. **Confidentiality and Trust**: Trust and confidentiality in handling mental health issues were recurrent themes, with suggestions to ensure that church members feel safe when discussing sensitive topics.

4. **Integration of Faith and Mental Health**: Some responses highlighted the importance of integrating biblical teachings with modern mental health practices, ensuring a holistic approach.

5. **Training for Clergy and Church Leaders**: There were calls for more training for clergy and church leaders to better understand and handle mental health issues, including suicide prevention.

Summary of Qualitative Responses

Theme	Frequency
Increased Education and Awareness	High
Support Groups and Counseling	High
Confidentiality and Trust	Moderate
Integration of Faith and Mental Health	Moderate
Training for Clergy and Church Leaders	Moderate

Conclusion

The analysis reveals that while church members appreciate the efforts made by their churches, there are clear areas for improvement. Increased education, support services, and better integration of faith and mental health practices are key areas highlighted by the respondents. Trust and confidentiality are also crucial factors that need to be addressed to ensure a supportive environment for those struggling with mental health issues.

Key Findings from the Suicide Survey for Black Church Members

Quantitative Findings

1. **Satisfaction with Church's Strategic Planning on Suicide Awareness and Prevention:**
   - A significant portion of respondents expressed disappointment with their church's current strategic planning regarding suicide awareness and prevention.

2. **Perception of Church's Seriousness about Mental Health:**
   - Responses varied, with some members feeling satisfied or very satisfied, while others felt neutral or disappointed, indicating mixed feelings about the church's approach to mental health.

3. **Trust in Clergy's Confidentiality Regarding Mental Health:**
   - Many respondents felt very satisfied or satisfied with the confidentiality maintained by clergy, suggesting a high level of trust in how personal information is handled.

4. **Church's Approach to the Topic of Suicide**:
   - There was a mix of responses, with some members feeling very satisfied, while others were neutral or very disappointed. This suggests differing views on whether the church addresses suicide with appropriate sensitivity and biblical context.

5. **Perception of Whether Church Considers Members' Input on Suicide Awareness and Prevention**:
   - Many respondents felt very satisfied that their input would be considered, though there were also neutral and disappointed responses, indicating room for improvement in inclusivity and consideration.

Qualitative Findings

From the analysis of the qualitative responses, several common themes emerged:

1. **Increased Education and Awareness Programs**:
   - Many respondents suggested that their churches need to implement more comprehensive education and awareness programs about mental health and suicide prevention.

2. **Support Groups and Counseling Services**:
   - A frequent recommendation was the establishment of support groups and accessible counseling services to provide ongoing mental health support to church members.

3. **Confidentiality and Trust**:
   - Ensuring confidentiality and building trust were highlighted as crucial factors. Respondents emphasized the importance of a safe space where mem-

bers can discuss their mental health issues without fear of judgment or breach of privacy.

4. **Integration of Faith and Mental Health**:
    o   There was a call for a balanced approach that integrates biblical teachings with modern mental health practices, promoting a holistic understanding of mental well-being.

5. **Training for Clergy and Church Leaders**:
    o   Respondents suggested that clergy and church leaders should receive more training to effectively address mental health issues and suicide prevention, ensuring they are well-equipped to support their congregations.

Summary

The survey results indicate that while there is trust in clergy confidentiality, there is a clear need for improved strategic planning and awareness programs regarding mental health and suicide prevention within the church. Respondents advocate for increased education, support services, integration of faith and mental health practices, and better training for church leaders. Addressing these areas can help create a more supportive and informed church environment for members dealing with mental health issues.

Detailed Summary Table

Theme	Common Suggestions
Increased Education and Awareness	Regular workshops, seminars, informational sessions about mental health and suicide prevention
Support Groups and Counseling	Establishment of support groups, accessible counseling services for ongoing mental health support
Confidentiality and Trust	Measures to ensure privacy of discussions, building trust with church leaders
Integration of Faith and Mental Health	Balanced approach combining biblical teachings with modern mental health practices
Training for Clergy and Church Leaders	More training for clergy and church leaders on mental health issues and suicide prevention

BIBLIOGRAPHY

Chapter One

1. The Harvard Crimson. Survey Reveals Eighty Percent of Protestant Ministers Without College, Graduate Training, Retrieved from https://www.thecrimson.com/article/1935/1/18/survey-reveals-eighty-percent-of-protestant/

2. Ibid

3. The Friends of Israel Gospel Ministry Inc. The Jewishness of Peter, Retrieved from https://israelmyglory.org/article/the-jewishness-of-peter/

4. Foster, J. D., & Ledbetter, M. F. (1987). Christian anti-psychology and the scientific method. *Journal of Psychology and Theology, 15*(1), 10–18.

5. Pacific Standard, The Rise of Biblical Counseling, Retrieved from, https://psmag.com/social-justice/evangelical-prayer-bible-religion-born-again-christianity-rise-biblical-counseling-89464

6. Marrs, "Christian Counseling The Past Generation." 32.

7. Pacific Standard, The Rise of Biblical Counseling, Retrieved from https://psmag.com/social-justice/evangelical-prayer-bible-religion-born-again-christianity-rise-biblical-counseling-89464

8. Ibid.

9. Seattle Neurocounseling, What is Neurocounseling, Retrieved from https://seattleneurocounseling.com/

10. Anita Phillips, *The Garden Within, The Garden Within:Where the War with Your Emotions Ends & Your Most Powerful Life Begins* (Nashville: Nelson Books, 2023), 97.

11. Baptist News Global, New Baylor Study, Retrieved from, https://baptistnews.com/article/new-baylor-study-finds-pastors-not-as-well-trained-in-trauma-care-as-they-need-to-be/

12. Ibid

13. Breeze, *Why People Choose Your Church*, Retrieved from https://www.breezechms.com/blog/why-people-choose-your-church

14. Frank A. Thomas, *Introduction into the Practice of African American Preaching* (Nashville: Abingdon Press, 2016),120.

15. Ibid., 121.

16. Ibid, 120

17. Stubbe DE, The Therapeutic Alliance, Retrieved from https://www.ncbi.nlm.nih.gov/pmc/articles/PMC6493237/

18. Samuel T. Gladding, *The Counseling Dictionary* (United States: Pearson, 2011), 154.

19. The American Association of Christian Counselors, Retrieved from https://aacc.net/2021/01/29/research-on-the-efficacy-of-christian-counseling/

20. Jackson, email message.

21. June Hunt, *Suicide Prevention: Hope When Life Seems Hopeless* (Dallas: Hope International Publishing 2023), 35.

22. Ibid

23. Khandicia Randolph, *The Black American Church: Leadership Dispensation and Challenges* (Meadville: Fulton Books, 2023),167.

24. Religion News Service, *Black Church Grapples with Mental Health*, Retrieved fromhttps://religionnews.com/2023/11/13/as-black-church-grapples-with-mental-health-clergy-are-both-subject-and-solution/

25. Dana Carson, *Is Christianity a White Man's Religion? How to Win African-American Males to the Kingdom of God* (Houston: Dana Carson Kingdom Ministries, 2014), 69.

Chapter Two

26. Banks, What is Biggie's Best-Selling Album, Retrieved from https://www.hotnewhiphop.com/733490-biggie-best-selling-album-life-after-death

27. University of Cambridge, 11 Hip/Hop Artists Who Had Something to Say About Mental Health, Retrieved from https://www.cam.ac.uk/stories/hiphoppsych

28. The Emory Wheel, *The History of Mental Health in Hip-hop*, Retrieved from https://emorywheel.com/a-history-of-mental-health-in-hip-hop/

29. T Magazine, Jay-Z & *Dean Baquet*, Retrieved from https://www.nytimes.com/interactive/2017/11/29/t-magazine/jay-z-dean-baquet-interview.html

30. Ibid

31. Natalie Y. Gutierrez, *The Pain We Carry: Healing from Complex PTSD for People of Color* (Oakland: New Harbinger Publications, 2022), 26.

32. The New York Times, Poverty and Inequality, Retrieved from https://www.nytimes.com/roomfordebate/2012/02/02/black-churches-and-a-new-generation-of-protest/poverty-and-inequality-remain-priorities-for-black-church-activism

33. Glaude, Jr., *Too Many Black Churches*, Retrieved from https://www.nytimes.com/roomfordebate/2014/06/25/has-capitalism-become-incompatible-with-christianity/too-many-black-churches-preach-the-gospel-of-greed

34. Psychol, Church and Family Support Networks, Retrieved from https://www.ncbi.nlm.nih.gov/pmc/articles/PMC5944602/

35. Ibid

36. *Michigan Chronicles, Black Church: We Need You, Retrieved from https://michiganchronicle.com/black-church-we-need-you/*

37. The Washington Post, *Black Americans Donate,* Retrieved from https://www.washingtonpost.com/business/2020/12/11/blacks-prioritize-philanthropy/

38. Hill Harper, *The Wealth Cure: Putting Money In Its Place* (USA: Gotham Books, 2011), 80.

39. Ibid., 82.

40. Dana Carson, *The Kingdom Culture, The Holy Spirit, & YOU!: Issues That Impact the Lives of Every Believer* (Houston: Dana Carson Kingdom Ministries, 2020), 173-174.

41. Dana Carson, *Why We Gather: Is Physical Gathering an Option?* (Houston: Kingdom Publishing, 2021), 172.

42. Ibid., 31.

43. Dr. Anita Phillips, *The Garden Within*, 39.

44. Psycom. 10 Biggest Barriers to Black Mental Health, Retrieved from, https://www.psycom.net/black-mental-health-barriers

45. The New York Times, Did Infamous Tuskegee Study Cause Lasting Mistrust of Doctors Among Blacks? Retrieved from https://www.nytimes.com/2016/06/18/upshot/long-term-mistrust-from-tuskegee-experiment-a-study-seems-to-overstate-the-case.html

46. Psycom, 10 Biggest Barriers to Black Mental Health Today, Retrieved from https://www.psycom.net/black-mental-health-barriers

47. Ibid

48. Jennifer Mullan, *Decolonizing Therapy: Oppression, Historical Trauma, and Politicizing Your Practice* (New York, NY: W. W Norton & Company, 2023), 84.

49. Ibid., 84-85.

50. Dr. Charles Moody, Jr., *Ecological Lynching: Perspectives on the Systeemtic Destruction of People of Color in America and the Responsibility of the Christian Church* (United States, 2020), 165-166.
51. Ibid.
52. Gutierrez, *The Pain We Carry*, 35
53. Bishop T. D. Jakes, Sermon, *"Hagar's Baby."*
54. Moody, Jr., *Ecological Lynching*, 171.

Chapter Three

55. Kalhan Rosenblatt, Kate Spade's Husband, Retrieved from https://www.nbcnews.com/news/us-news/fashion-designer-kate-spade-found-dead-her-new-york-apartment-n880201
56. Ibid.
57. Market Realist, What Was Fashion Designer Kate Spade's Net Worth? Retrieved from https://market-realist.com/what-was-kate-spades-net-worth/
58. Kalhan Rosenblatt, Kate Spade's Husband, Retrieved from https://www.nbcnews.com/news/us-news/fashion-designer-kate-spade-found-dead-her-new-york-apartment-n880201
59. Ibid.
60. Ibid.
61. Ibid.
62. Kobe Campbell, *Why Am I Like This: How to Break Cycles, Heal From Trauma, and Restore Your Faith* (Nashville Tennessee: Thomas Nelson, 2023), 5.
63. Kalhan Rosenblatt, Kate Spade's Husband, Retrieved from https://www.nbcnews.com/news/us-news/fashion-designer-kate-spade-found-dead-her-new-york-apartment-n880201
64. Ibid.
65. Ibid.

66. Cosby & Poussaint, *Come on People:On the Path from Victims to Victors* (Nashville: Tennessee: Thomas Nelson, 2007), 10.

67. Ibid.

68. Knowledge at Wharton, *Conspicuous Consumption and Race: Who Spends More*, Retrieved from https://knowledge.wharton.upenn.edu/podcast/knowledge-at-wharton-podcast/conspicuous-consumption-and-race-who-spends-more-on-what/

69. Terrie M. Williams, *Black Pain: It Just Looks Like We're Not Hurting* (New York, NY: Scribner, 2008) 119.

70. Pamela Robinson, *The Color of Hope:African American Mental Health in the Church* (United States: Season Press, 2020), 8.

71. The Professional Counselor. *Racism, Family Secrets & the African American Experience.* Retrieved from https://tpcjournal.nbcc.org/video-review-racism-family-secrets-and-the-african-american-experience/

72. Mullan, *Decolonizing Therapy.*,106.

73. Gutierrez, *The Pain We Carry.*, 81.

74. Williams, *Black Pain: It Just Looks Like We're Not Hurting*, 206.

75. T.D. Jakes, *Help Me, I've Fallen and I Can't Get Up* (Shippensburg, PA: Destiny Image Publishers, 1995), 24.

76. Rheeda Walker, *The Unapologetic Guide to Black Mental Health: Navigate an Unequal System, Learn Tools for Emotional Wellness, and Get the Help You Deserve* (Oakland, CA: New Harbinger Publications, 2020), 40.

77. Mary-Frances Winters, *Black Fatigue: How Racism Erodes the Mind, Body, and Spirit* (Oakland, CA:Berrett-Koehler Publishers, 2020), 144.

78. Anxiety & Depression Association of America. *The Black Church: Our Refuge, Our Mental Health*, Retrieved from https://adaa.org/learn-from-us/from-the-experts/blog-posts/conference-consumer-professional/black-church-our-refuge

79. Celebrity Net Worth, Henry Louis Gates, Jr., Retrieved from https://www.celebrity-networth.com/richest-celebrities/authors/henry-louis-gates-jr-net-worth/

80. The New York Times, Harvard Professor Jailed; Officer Accused of Bias, Retrieved from https://www.nytimes.com/2009/07/21/us/21gates.html

81. Ibid

82. Ibid

83. Ibid

84. Christianity Today, *The Legacy of Women in the Black Church*, Retrieved from https://www.christianitytoday.com/women-leaders/2016/february/legacy-of-women-in-black-church.html

85. Parks, *Fierce Angels: The Strong Black Woman in American Life and Culture* (New York: One World Books, 2010), 115.

86. Boston University, Study: Black Women, Aged 18-54 Years, Retrieved from https://www.bumc.bu.edu/camed/2023/10/04/bu-study-black-women-aged-18-65-years-have-highest-suicide-risk-among-women/

87. Ibid.

88. Ibid.

89. Parks, *Fierce Angels: The Strong Black Woman in American Life and Culture*, 157.

90. Ibid., 142.

91. Ibid., 158.

92. Ibid., 167-168.

93. Walker, *The Unapologetic Guide to Black Mental Health*, 27.

Chapter Four

94. Religious New Service, As Black Church Grapples with mental health, clergy are both subject and solution, Retrieved from https://religionnews.

com/2023/11/13/as-black-church-grapples-with-mental-health-clergy-are-both-subject-and-solution/

95.   Ibid.

96.   The Christian Recorder, *Psychology & Problematic Preaching: The Black Church and What to Preach After the Pandemic*, Retrieved from https://etd.ohiolink.edu/acprod/odb_etd/ws/send_file/send?accession=ohiou1679939983272928&disposition=inline

97.   Psychology Today, *Why Your Pastor Can't Be Your Therapist*, Retrieved from https://www.psychology-today.com/us/blog/inside-intimacy/202309/why-your-pastor-cant-be-your-therapist

98.   Ibid.

99.   Dr. Thema, *Meet Dr. Thema*, Retrieved from https://drthema.com/

100. Black Psychologist of America, *History*, Retrieved from https://blackpsychiatrists.org/about

101. Shondaland, *How Dr. Thema Bryant Is Seeking to Shake Up Psychology*, Retrieved from https://www.shondaland.com/live/body/a43029410/how-dr-thema-bryant-is-seeking-to-shake-up-psychology/

102. Ibid.

103. BET, *Black Pastors Say They Are Overwhelmed With People Coming to Them for Mental Health Care*, Retrieved from, https://www.bet.com/article/m8zegc/black-pastors-say-they-are-overwhelmed-with-people-coming-to-them-for-mental-health-care

104. Religion Dispatches, A Pastor's Suicide: Addressing Mental Health in Black Churches, Retrieved from https://religiondispatches.org/a-pastors-suicide-addressing-mental-health-in-black-churches/

105. Ibid

106. Robert C. Rogers and Taunya M. Tinsley, "Black Pastor's Experience of Occupational and Life Stress During COVID-19 in the USA," *Journal of Religion and Health* 63, (2024): 685.

107. Ibid.

108. Williams, *Black Pain: It Just Looks Like We're Not Hurting*, 3.

109. Thema Bryant, *Homecoming: Healing Trauma to Reclaim Your Authentic Self* (United States: Penguin Random House, 2022), 15.

110. Williams, *Black Pain: It Just Looks Like We're Not Hurting*, 3.

111. Ibid.

112. Ibid.

113. Foxy, 5 Black Celebrities That Took Their Own Life, Retrieved from https://foxync.com/playlist/black-celebrities-committed-suicide/item/1

114. Paul A. Hauck, *Overcoming Frustration and Anger* (Philadelphia, PA: Westminster Press, 1974), 29.

115. The New York Times, Donnie Hathaway, 33, Pop and Blues Singer, Dead in Hotel Plunge, Retrieved from https://www.nytimes.com/1979/01/15/archives/donny-hathaway-33-pop-and-blues-singer-dead-in-hotel-plunge-hit.html

116. Mayo Clinic, *Schizophrenia*, Retrieved from https://www.mayoclinic.org/diseases-conditions/schizophrenia/symptoms-causes/syc-20354443

117. Ibid.

118. Newspaper, *Donny Hathaway to be buried in St. Louis*, Retrieved from https://www.newspapers.com/article/st-louis-post-dispatch-donny-hathaway-t/8307063/

119. Williams, *Black Pain: It Just Looks Like We're Not Hurting*, 21.

120. Dibabetic, Divabetic Remembers Phyllis Hyman, Retrieved from https://divabetic.org/2018/01/24/divabetic-remembers-phyllis-hyman/

121. Cleveland Clinic, Bipolar Disorder, Retrieved from https://my.clevelandclinic.org/health/diseases/9294-bipolar-disorder

122. Ibid.

123. Time, *Megachurch Pastor and Mental Health Advocate Jarrid Wilson Dies by Suicide*, Retrieved from https://time.com/5674636/megachurch-pastor-jarrid-wilson-dies-suicide/

124. Williams, *Black Pain: It Just Looks Like We're Not Hurting*, 19.

125. Dana Carson, *Kingdom Exegesis: The New Testament* (Houston, Texas: Dana Carson Kingdom Ministries, 2017), 34.

126. Eric Mason, Urban Apologetics: *Restoring Black Dignity With the Gospel* (Grand Rapids: Zondervan, 2021), 27.

127. Clayborne Carson, *The Autobiography of Martin Luther King, Jr.*, New York, NY: Grand Central Publishing, 1998), 184.

128. Ibid., 223.

129. The Seattle Times, IHOP: *'Zero tolerance' for server's treatment of Black teens*, Retrieved from, https://www.seattletimes.com/business/ihop-apologizes-to-black-teens-forced-to-prepay-for-meal/

130. The Denver Post, Denver Chili's refused to serve Black family unless they paid in advance, lawsuit alleges, Retrieved from https://www.denverpost.com/2023/12/06/lawsuit-racial-discrimination-chilis-restaurant-denver/

131. Camille Lloyd and Courtney Brown, One in Five Black Students Report Discrimination Experiences, Retrieved from https://news.gallup.com/poll/469292/one-five-black-students-report-discrimination-experiences.aspx

132. U.S. Bureau of Labor Statistics, Retrieved from https://www.bls.gov/cps/cpsaat03.htm

133. Institute for Social Research Center for Political Studies: *University of Michigan, How Do White Churches Talk About Racism*, Retrieved from https://cpsblog.isr.umich.edu/?p=3197

Chapter Five

134. Raphael G.Warnock, *The Divided Mind of the Black Church: Theology, Piety & Public Witness* (New York: New York University Press, 2014), 9.

135. Ibid., 24.

136. Mullan, *Decolonizing Therapy*, 140-141.

137. Ibid., 145.

138. Ibid.,144-145.

139. Ibid., 141-142

140. Ibid., 145.

141. Ibid., 146.

142. Warnock, *The Divided Mind of the Black Church*, 27.

143. Ibid., 28.

144. Williams, *Black Pain: It Just Looks Like We're Not Hurting*, 198.

145. Joy Degruy, *Post Traumatic Slave Syndrome: America's Legacy of Enduring Injury & Healing* (United States: Uptone Press, 2005), 58.

146. Cosby and Poussaint, *Come on People: On the Path from Victims to Victors*, p. 73.

147. Dr. Charles A. Moody, Jr., *Ecological Lynching*, 215-216.

148. Poussaint, *Come on People*, 195.

149. 149. Kaitlyn Washburn, *"Black people exposed to gun violence more likely to deal with suicidal thoughts, says new study,"* Retrieved from https://healthjournalism.org/blog/2024/02/black-people-exposed-to-gun-violence-more-likely-to-deal-with-suicidal-thoughts-says-new-study/

150. Poussaint, *Come on People*, 196.

151. Allen Lipscomb, *"Sexual Healing: How Racialized Black Males Use Sex to Cope with Stress, Loss and Separation,"* The Journal of Sociology & Social Welfare: Vol. 46: Iss. 1, Article 3. DOI: https://doi.org/10.15453/0191-5096.4134

152. A. L. Reynolds, *Do Black Women Hate Black Men?* (Mamaronek, NY: Hasting House, 1994), 9, quoted in Dana Carson, *Is Christianity the White Man's Religion* (Texas: Dana Carson Kingdom Ministries, 2014), 129.

153. DL stands for Down Low.

154. Washington Post, *Why Some Black Men Prefer the Down Low and What It Says About the Black Church in America,* Retrieved from https://www.washingtonpost.com/national/religion/why-some-black-men-prefer-the-down-low-and-what-it-says-about-the-black-church-in-america/2015/09/04/59788754-533b-11e5-b225-90edbd49f362_story.html

155. Hiv.gov, What is the Impact of HIV on Racial and Ethnic Minorities in the U.S. ?, Retrieved from https://www.hiv.gov/hiv-basics/overview/data-and-trends/impact-on-racial-and-ethnic-minorities

156. Ibid.

157. NBC News, Opinion: 'Don't Ask, Don't Tell' in the Black Church, Retrieved from https://www.nbcnews.com/feature/nbc-out/opinion-don-t-ask-don-t-tell-black-church-n747096

158. The Trevor Project, Mental Health of Black Trangender and Nonbinary Young People, Retrieved from https://www.thetrevorproject.org/research-briefs/mental-health-of-black-transgender-and-non-binary-young-people-feb-2023/

159. Pew Research Center, *Recent Surge in U.S. Drug Overdose Death has Hit Black Men the Hardest,* Retrieved from https://www.pewresearch.org/short-reads/2022/01/19/recent-surge-in-u-s-drug-over-dose-deaths-has-hit-black-men-the-hardest/

160. MEDPAGETODAY, *Suicide Rates Among Black Women Rose Over 2 Decades,* Retrieved from https://www.medpagetoday.com/psychiatry/generalpsychiatry/107665

161. Williams, *Black Pain: It Just Looks Like We're Not Hurting*, 37-38.

162. Scrutton, *Christianity and Depression*, 50.

163. Winters, *Black Fatigue*, 117-118.

164. Williams, *Black Pain: It Just Looks Like We're Not Hurting*, 71.

165. Ibid.

166. Health City, Binge Eating Disorders Among Black Women Are Going Underdiagnosed, Retrieved from https://live-healthcity2.pantheonsite.io/binge-eating-disorders-among-black-women-are-going-undiagnosed/

167. Winters, *Black Fatigue*, 116.

168. Ibid., 119.

169. Williams, *Black Pain*, 50.

170. Ruth King, *Healing Rage: Women Making Inner Peace Possible*, (New York, NY: Gotham Books, 2007), 4.

171. Winters, *Black Fatigue*, 122.

172. Speakola, Malcolm X: 'The Most Disrespected Person in America, is the Black Woman', Speech to Women, Retrieved from https://speakola.com/political/malcolm-x-speech-to-black-women-1962

173. Campbell, *Why Am I Like This?*, 41.

174. Williams, *Black Pain*, 125-126.

175. Tamar Mendelson, *Child and Adolescent Psychiatric Clinics of North America*, quoted in Jennifer Mullan, *Decolonizing Therapy*, 343.

Chapter Six

176. Jackie Mccullough, *I Hate My Life: Winning the War Against Covetousness & Discontentment* (United States: Proclamation Publishing, 2019), 17.

177. Antonieta Contreras, *Traumatization and Its Aftermath: A Systemic Approach to Understanding and Treating Trauma Disorders* (New York: Routledge, 2024),12.

178. Mental Health America, Racial Trauma, Retrieved from https://www.mhanational.org/racial-trauma

179. Resmaa Menakem, *My Grandmother's Hands* (Los Vegas, NV: Central Recovery Press, 2017),14.

180. Mullan, *Decolonizing Therapy*, 42.

181. Degruy, *Post Traumatic Slave Syndrome*, 105.

182. Moody, Jr., Ecological Lynching, 73-74.

183. Ibid., 75.

184. Menakem, *Grandmother's Hands*, 15.

185. Bryant, *Homecoming*, 38.

186. Campbell, *Why Am I Like This?*, 48.

187. Andrew Billingsley, *Climbing Jacob's Ladder.* (New York, NY: Touchstone, 1992), 61, 88, quoted in Dana Carson, *Is Christianity the White Man's Religion?* (Texas: Dana Carson Kingdom Ministries, 2014, 99.

188. Dr. Jennifer Sweeton, *Here's Your Brain on Trauma*, Retrieved from https://www.jennifersweeton.com/heres-your-brain-on-trauma/

189. Jennifer Sweeton, *Eight Key Areas of Mental Health and Illness* (United States: W. W. Norton & Company, 2021), 5.

190. Ibid., 6.

191. Ibid.

192. Ibid., 36.

193. Ibid., 38.

194. Ibid., 119.

195. Ibid.

196. Ibid., 52.

197. Ibid., 53.

198. Ibid.

199. Phillips, *the Garden Within*, 103.

200. Ibid.

201. Sweeton, *Eight Key Brain Areas of Mental Health*, 72.

202. Ibid.

203. Ibid., 79.

204. Ibid., 17

205. Ibid., 19.

206. Ibid., 20.

207. Phillips, *the Garden Within*, 137.

208. Sweeton, *Eight Brain Areas of Mental Health*, 92.

209. Ibid., 30.

210. Singersroom, Mary Mary's Erica Talks Near Stroke, Health Care, Retrieved from https://singersroom. com/content/2013-03-24/mary-marys-erica-talks-near-stroke-health-scare/

211. Ibid.

212. Phillips, *The Garden Within*, 189.

213. Menakem, *Grandmother's Hands*, 138.

214. Ibid., 147.

215. Duane P. Schultz and Sydney Ellen Schultz, *Theories of Personality* (Belmont, CA: Wadsworth, 2009), 303.

216. Dr. Timothy Murphy, *The Christ Cure: 10 Biblical Ways to Heal From Trauma, Tragedy*, and PTSD (West Palm Beach, FL: Humanix Books, 2023), 24-25.

217. William H. Grier and Prince M.Cobbs, *Black Rage: Two Black Psychiatrists Reveal the Full Dimensions of the Inner Conflicts and the Desperation of Black Life in the United States* (United States: Basic Books, 1968), 24.

218. Walker, *The Unapologetic Guide to Black Mental Health*, 43.

219. Damond T. Holt & Dr. Carlian W. Dawson, *Black Trauma: What Happens to Us* (Columbia, SC: Independently Published, 2024), 27-28.

220. Williams, *Black Pain*, 249.

221. Ibid., pp.209-210.

222. Dr. F. Poussaint & Dr. Amy Alexander, *Lay My Burden Down: Suicide and the Mental Health Crisis Among African Americans*, 19.

223. Ibid.

224. Ibid., 18.

225. Holt & Dawson, *Black Trauma*, 139.

Chapter Seven

226. The New York Times, 2 Charged in Mid-Sermon Robbery of Bejeweled Brooklyn Bishop, Retrieved from, https://www.nytimes.com/2022/09/28/nyregion/bishop-lamor-whitehead-arrests.html

227. Robinson, *The Color of Hope*: African American Mental Health in the Church (NC: Season Press, 2020),8-9.

228. Tate, *The Decline in Black Men's Church Attendance: The Role of the Male Presence in the Family* (TN: JAT Publications, 2024), 77.

229. 229. Ibid., 25.

230. Ibid., 26.

231. Carson, *Is Christianity the White Man's Religion*, 121.

232. https://dictionary.cambridge.org/us/dictionary/english/embittered

233. Victor M. Erlich, *Modern Psychology in the Ancient Bible: Ethical Monotheism in the Hebrew Mind* (Charleston, SC: Palmetto Publishing, 2021), 91-92.

234. Cosby & Poussaint, *Come on People*, 198.

235. T. D. Jakes, *He-Motions: Even Strong Men Struggle* (New York, NY: The Berkley Publishing Group, 2004), 171.

236. Charlamagne, *Shook One: Anxiety Playing Tricks On Me* (New York, NY: Touchstone, 2018), 76.

237. Ibid., 77.

238. Ibid.

239. Menakem, *My Grandmother's Hands*, 97-98.

240. Ibid., 102-103.

241. Ibid., 98.

242. Joseph N. Cooper, Why Are Black Males Supported Only When They're Athletes?, Retrieved from https://www.bostonglobe.com/magazine/2019/08/21/why-

are-black-males-only-supported-when-they-athletes/
QwspMiHYgujEvhWi3VSI7L/story.html

243. Grier & Cobbs, *Black Rage*, 58-59.

244. Ibid.

245. Jason Wilson, *Cry Like a Man: Fighting for Freedom from Emotional Incarceration* (Colorado Springs, CO: David C. Cook, 2019), 50-51.

246. Wilson, *Cry Like Like a Man*, 93

247. George D. McKinney, *The New Slave Masters* (Colorado Springs, CO: Cook Communication Ministries, 2005), 69.

248. Michelle Alexander, *The New Jim Crow: Mass Incarceration in the Age of Colorblindness*, (NY: The New Press, 2020), 26.

249. Alton R. Kirk, *Black Suicide: The Tragic Reality of America's Deadliest Secret* (Silver Spring, MD: The Beckham Publishing Group, 22009), 42-43.

250. American Oversight, The January 6 Attack On the U.S. Capitol, Retrieved from https://www.americanoversight.org/investigation/the-january-6-attack-on-the-u-s-capitol

251. Ronald S. Martin, *White Fear: How the Browning of America is Making White Folks Lose Their Minds* (Dallas, TX: Benbella), 13.

252. Holt & Dawson, *Black Trauma*, 23.

Chapter Eight

253. Andrews, Willard, Demarest, Hull. *The Kingdom Life: A Practical Theology of Discipleship and Spiritual Formation* (Colorado Springs, CO: NavPress, 2010), 29.

254. Obery M. Hendricks, Jr., *The Politics of Jesus: Rediscovering the True Revolutionary Nature of Jesus' Teaching and How They Have Been Corrupted* (NY: Three Leaves Press), 7-8.

255. Jemar Tisby, *The Color of Compromise: The Truth About the American Church's Complicity in Racism* (Grand Rapids, MI: Zondervan, 2019), 19.

256. Mason, *Urban Apologetics*, p.51.

257. Pew Research Center, Faith Among Black Americans, Retrieved from https://www.pewresearch.org/religion/2021/02/16/faith-among-black-americans/

258. Ibid.

259. Mason, *Urban Apologetics*, pp.98-99.

260. Al Sharpton & Anthony Walton, *Go and Tell Pharaoh: The Autobiography of the Reverend Al Sharpton*, (New York, NY: Doubleday, 1996), 23.

261. Degruy, *Post Traumatic Slave Syndrome*, p.109.

262. Ibid., p.110.

263. Ibid.

264. Ibid.

265. Cosby & Poussaint, *Come on People*, p. 196.

266. USA Today, Fact Check: Rates of White-on-White and Black-on-Black crime are similar, Retrieved from https://www.usatoday.com/story/news/fact-check/2020/09/29/fact-check-meme-shows-incorrect-homicide-stats-race/5739522002/

267. National Alliance of Mental Illness. Why Self-Esteem is Important for Mental Health, Retrieved from https://www.nami.org/family-member-caregivers/why-self-esteem-is-important-for-mental-health/

268. Poussaint & Alexander, *Lay My Burden Down: Suicide and the Mental Health Crisis Among African Americans* (Boston, MA: Beacon Press, 2000), 46.

269. Rose Jackson-Beavers & Jermine D. Alberty. *Bottled Up Inside: African American Teens and Depression*, (Florissant, MO: Priority Books), 35.

Chapter Nine

270. Craig J. Bryan, *Rethinking Suicide: Why Prevention Fails, and How We Can Do Better* (New York, NY: Oxford University Press, 2022), 41.

271. The Guardian. In Quarantine With An Abuser: Surge in Domestic Violence Reports Linked to Coronavirus, Retrieved from https://www.theguardian.com/us-news/2020/apr/03/coronavirus-quarantine-abuse-domestic-violence

272. Joshua L. Mitchell, *Black Millennials & the Church: Meet Me Where I Am* (Valley Forge, PA: Judson Press, 2018),14.

273. Allashia Smith-Harris, *Hidden: Mental Illness Hides Out in the Church: A Practical Guide to Identify and Manage Mental Illness in Your Congregation,* (Seattle, WA: Kindle Direct Publishing), 11.

274. Campbell, *Why Am I Like This*, p.174.

275. Edward M. Hallowell, *Worry: Hope and Help for a Common Condition* (NewYork: The Random House Publishing Group, 2002), 300-301.

276. Nicole Hannah-Jones, *The 1619 Project: A New Origin Story* (New York: Oneworld, 2021), 339.

277. Ibid

278. Hunt, *Suicide Prevention*, p. 98.

279. Lewis Brogdon, *Dying to Lead: The Disturbing Trend of Clergy Suicide* (United Stress: Seymour Press, 2014), 32.

280. Ibid., p.27.

281. Ibid., p.26.

282. Bryan, *Rethinking Suicide*, 135.

283. Ibid., 84.

284. Ibid., 34.

285. Ibid., 34-35.

286. Dave Miller, *Roman Jailer's Attempted Suicide.* Retrieved from https://apologeticspress.org/roman-jailers-attempted-suicide/

287. H. Norman Wright. *The Complete Guide to Crisis & Trauma Counseling: What to Do and Say When It Matters Most!* (Bloomington, MN: Bethany House Publishers, 2011), 288.

288. Ibid.

289. Ibid.

290. Tony V. Lewis. *Pastoral Counseling: An Introduction to Pastoral Care* (Ramona, CA: Vision Publishing, 2020), 168.

291. Mark R. McMinn. *Psychology, Theology, and Spirituality in Christian Counseling* (United States: Tyndale, 2011), 98.

292. Craig J. Bryan and M. David Rudd. *Brief Cognitive Behavioral Therapy for Suicide Prevention* (New York:Guilford Press, 2018), 4.

293. Ibid.

294. Ibid.

295. Ibid.

296. Ibid.

297. Ibid.

298. Ibid., 5.

299. Ibid.

300. LaVerne Hanes Collins. *Overlooked: Counselor Insights for the Unspoken Issues in Black American Life* (Lanham, MD, Rowman & Littlefield, 2024), 28.

301. Craig J. Bryan. *Cognitive Behavioral Therapy for Preventing Suicide Attempts: A Guide to Brief Treatments Across Clinical Settings* (New York, NY:Routledge, 2015), 15.

302. Ibid., 23.

303. Ibid., 16.

304. Ibid., 16-19.

305. Bryan, *Brief Cognitive Behavioral Therapy*, 8.

306. Ibid., 7.

307. W.M. Schmitz, M.H. Allen, B.N. Feldman, N. J. Gutin, D.R. Jahn, P. M. Kleespies, P. Quinnett, & S. Simpson. Preventing Suicide Through Improved Training in Suicde Risk Assessment and Care: An American Association of Suicidology Task Force Report Addressing Serious Gaps in U.S. Mental Health Training. *Suicide and Life Theratening Behavior*, 42, 292-304.

About the Author

Dr. Curtis T. Bracy is a Kingdom-driven preacher, commissioned by the King of Kings to deliver the Christ-centered message of the Kingdom of God. He holds a Bachelor's Degree in Psychology from Kean University and a Master's in Counseling with a focus on Marriage, Family, and Couples Counseling from Pillar College. Dr. Bracy earned his Doctorate in Christian Counseling & Psychology from the Christian Bible Institute & Seminary and is a licensed Associate Counselor in New Jersey.

As a board-certified Christian counselor and licensed Christian marriage and family therapist, Dr. Bracy is also certified in crisis and suicide prevention, advanced EMDR therapy, and Neuropsychotherapy. In his practice, he specializes in areas including self-esteem, Black trauma, racism, and suicidality.

Beyond his therapeutic work, Dr. Bracy is an adjunct professor of Suicide Prevention at the National Association of Christian Counselors (NACC) and Christian Bible Institute & Seminary. He is the author of several impactful books, including *Christ Confident, Temptation,* and *Controversial for the Kingdom.*

A dedicated member of the American Counseling Association, National Association of Black Counselors (NABC) and the American Association of Suicidality, Dr. Bracy's ministry reflects the words of King Jesus: "I must preach the good news of the Kingdom of God." His life's mission is to guide individuals toward healing and transformation through the power of Christ.

The Kingdom Collection

*Christ Confident: Finally Placing Our
Confidence in the Right One*

Temptation: Your Destiny Signal

*Controversial for the Kingdom of Christ:
You Can't Be Anointed Without It*

Check out more at <u>www.curtisbracy.com</u>

www.ingramcontent.com/pod-product-compliance
Lightning Source LLC
Chambersburg PA
CBHW050502160726
48003CB00001B/120